12·99

History & Guide

SOUTHALL AND HANWELL

942.19

Southall e Hanwell history   Oakes, J

History & Guide

SOUTHALL AND HANWELL

Jonathan Oates

TEMPUS

First published 2003

Tempus Publishing Limited
The Mill, Brimscombe Port,
Stroud, Gloucestershire, GL5 2QG

British Library Cataloguing in Publication Data.
A catalogue record for this book is available from the British Library.

ISBN 0 7524 2638 9

Typesetting and origination by Tempus Publishing Limited
Printed in Great Britain by Midway Colour Print, Wiltshire.

Contents

Acknowledgements

I would like to thank the London Borough of Ealing for the use of most of the photographs reproduced here. I would also like to thank the following for reading this work and for their helpful suggestions: Mr D. Blackwell, Mr E. Crouchman, Mr P. Fitzmaurice, Miss M. Gooding, Dr P. Hounsell, Mr G. Twyman. Any errors, of course, are mine alone. Help on the Walking Tour section was gratefully received from Mrs Oates and Mr Panther.

This book is dedicated to the late Ted Crouchman, lifelong resident of Southall and assiduous local historian and researcher.

The vibrant window display of a Southall jewellery shop.

Introduction

This new history of these two ancient Middlesex parishes needs a few introductory paragraphs. As some readers may know, there are already several existing histories of Hanwell and Southall. The most recent is Peter Hounsell's *Ealing and Hanwell Past*, published in 1991, though this chiefly covers only nineteenth-century history. The only narrative history of Hanwell is Sir Montagu Sharpe's *Bygone Hanwell*, which is not an easy volume to digest, and, in any case, concludes its story in the year 1885. *Southall: 830-1982* was written by Richard Meads in 1982, and is often inaccurate and anecdotal, and the coverage given to many aspects of Southall history, including that of post-war immigration, is unsatisfactory. Paul Kirwan's *Southall: A Brief History* is, in many ways, better, but does not deal with Southall after amalgamation in 1965. The volumes of the *Victoria County History: Middlesex* which cover Hanwell and Southall (III and IV), are excellent, but, like Peter Hounsell's book, are thematic in their treatment of (mainly) social and economic history.

Unlike the books just mentioned, this is a narrative history of both parishes, comparing and contrasting where applicable. Apart from chapter four, which covers the canals and railways, the structure is chronological. Differing from many local histories, this book also considers the interplay between national history with local history, as well as tackling purely local concerns. It examines local government, the economy; farming, shops, trade and industry, religion, crime, leisure, transport, wars and civil commotion, and other aspects of life in Hanwell and Southall. Above all, though, it is about people, without whom there would be no history. It begins in prehistoric times and ends in 2001. The bulk of the book covers the eighteenth to the twentieth centuries. This is, however, in no way a comprehensive account, but a survey of some of the major points of each district's history.

There are a number of similarities between Southall and Hanwell. They were adjoining parishes in the Hundred of Elthorne in the county of Middlesex. The Oxford Road, later the Uxbridge Road, has run from London through both since the Middle Ages, as the principal western thoroughfare from the capital. More recently, both the Grand Junction Canal and the Great Western Railway run through both parishes between the capital and the West of England. Until the late nineteenth century, they were both small, sparsely populated and mainly agricultural parishes, in common with many others in Middlesex.

From the late nineteenth century these two parishes began to differ

in essential character. Southall became industrialized, Hanwell did not, and became a commuter suburb, very much in the shadow of Ealing. It was during this century that Southall's population overtook that of Hanwell. Whereas Hanwell was amalgamated with Ealing in 1926, Southall achieved borough status in 1936. After 1945, Southall became a magnet for immigrants, mostly from the Indian sub-continent.

However, in 1965, the two ancient parishes began to have more similarities than differences. Firstly, Southall joined Ealing and Acton to become the London Borough of Ealing; thus Hanwell and Southall were now jointly administered from Ealing. With the recessions of the 1970s, Southall lost some of its industrial character, thus lessening the contrast. Thirdly, both places attracted overseas immigrants, though more so in Southall than Hanwell.

Before the historical treatment is attempted, a few brief paragraphs will summarize some of the geographical and geological facts about the two places.

Hanwell is a long, thin parish, almost three miles from north to south and about one third of a mile west to east. It is bordered on the north and the west by the River Brent, to the east by Ealing and to the south by Brentford. Originally New (or West) Brentford formed the southern part of Hanwell (Old Brentford was part of Ealing). In total, Hanwell's acreage was 992. This book does not cover New Brentford.

The topography of Hanwell is mostly flat, but there are some gradients. The steepest is that north of the Uxbridge Road to the summit of Cuckoo Hill, which is where the Greenford Avenue now runs. St Mary's church also stands on a spur overlooking the Brent Valley. The soil is mixed; there is both gravel and clay.

The origins of Hanwell's name are hotly disputed, the most commonly accepted one is that it springs from two words, 'Hanna' and 'welle', meaning Hanna's Well. Other versions include 'Hean weal', meaning 'the slaughter on the hill' – an allusion to the alleged 'Battle of Bloody Croft' as noted in chapter one, or 'Han' meaning hen (Hen's Well) or 'Han' meaning boundary stone and 'well' meaning a spring.

Unlike Hanwell, Southall is basically square; with Greenford to the north, Hanwell to the east, Heston to the south and Hayes to the west. The River Brent runs north to south to form a border between Hanwell and Southall, while the Yeading Brook forms the western border with Hayes. It is a far bigger parish than Hanwell; its acreage in the 1860s was 2461. Minor boundary changes occurred over the years, so that by 1961 it measured 2,608 acres.

As is the case with Hanwell, the parish is flat, though even more so. There is nothing higher than fifty feet above sea level. Again, as in Hanwell, the soil is mostly gravel and clay.

Southall, it must be remembered, has its origins as a hamlet of the division of Norwood, in the parish of Hayes (the parish was, apart from being an ecclesiastical jurisdiction, an important unit of civil government from the sixteenth until the late nineteenth century). In fact, it is more accurate to speak of Norwood, rather than Southall until the later nineteenth century, and this practice will be used here. It will be noted wherever Norwood the hamlet is meant; otherwise Norwood can be taken to mean the whole division. Norwood was first mentioned in AD 832, Southall not until the twelfth century. Norwood was first spelt 'Northuuda' in 832, and means 'north wood'. Southall was first mentioned in 1198 as 'Suhaull', meaning 'south nook', presumably to distinguish it from Northolt.

Jonathan Oates, June 2002

CHAPTER 1
Origins to 1485

We know very little about the centuries of Southall and Hanwell's history before the sixteenth century, since there is scarcely any surviving evidence (written or otherwise) for what were two small Saxon villages. What follows is a summary of this evidence.

The first known life (and probably death) in what is now Southall was that of a woolly mammoth, the remains of which were discovered in 1887. Archaeological evidence, in the form of long pointed stone implements suggests that the beast was hunted by Stone Age men towards the end of the Pleistocene period, which could be anything between 25,000-50,000 years ago. Since sharp stone implements were found in contact with a bone, it is probable that the hunt was successful. It would seem that the Thames' banks were further north than they are now, and that the land on which Southall is now situated was marshy, just north of the river. The published account of these remains was written by John Allen Brown, an Ealing antiquarian.

There is other evidence of Stone Age Man in what is now Southall and Hanwell. Flint axes, six-and-a-half inches long, were found during excavations for Southall Gasworks. Neolithic flints were found near Norwood Green. Palaeolithic axe heads were also discovered in gravel pits opposite Elthorne Avenue, belonging to Mr Seward of Hanwell in 1910.

Moving forward in time, Bronze Age pottery remains were found in Seward's Pit in Hanwell, suggesting a settlement, at least, in this district long before the Romans invaded these isles. In 1897, a bronze hoard was discovered in a Southall brick-field. This included four palstaves or axe heads, a ring and leaden celts. Furthermore, during excavations for the Grand Junction Canal between Slough and Southall in 1900, a bronze axe head was discovered, dating from about 1200 BC. Coins and Iron Age pottery have been found at Hanwell Park, between what is now Greenford Avenue and Copley Close.

One of the ancient monuments in Hanwell is the Sarsen stone which is now in Elthorne Park. This stone, measuring 3ft 7in by 2ft 9in was carried to Hanwell by the old river bed. It was found during excavations for the building of Townholme Crecent in the 1900s and had probably been in its former position for thousands of years.

Seward's Pit, Hanwell, site of prehistoric discoveries, 1910.

Sarsen Stone, Elthorne Park, Hanwell.

Roman coins and pottery have been found in Hanwell Park, but there were no known Roman villas here. This may be evidence of a temporary encampment, rather than any permanent settlement.

It is probable that Hanwell and Southall originated in Anglo-Saxon times as permanent settlements carved out of the forests which covered Middlesex before the Norman Conquest. Certainly the will of the Saxon priest Werherd of AD 832 mentions 120 acres of land and property in Norwood, which he gave to the Archbishop of Canterbury, who was lord of the manor. Remains of ten fifth or sixth century Saxon warriors have been found in Hanwell, on the site of what is now Oaklands Road school. They were wearing woven garments and carried spears. About fifty spearheads were found nearby. It has been suggested by Sharpe that these skeletons of warriors indicate a battle between Britons and Saxons, the Battle of Bloody Croft, as some writers have called it. This seems likely to be a piece of romantic history as there is no suggestion that these men were killed in battle.

Saxon pottery has been found near Dormers Wells Farm and near to what is now the Boston Road. Three round Saxon brooches of gilt bronze have been found in Hanwell, on the site of the county school.

West Saxon fibulae
(coins) found at Hanwell.

We know very little else of Hanwell or Norwood in Saxon times. The two Saxon charters which refer to Hanwell are now thought to be forgeries. The apparently older one, of AD 959, was a grant of land from Archbishop Dunstan to Westminster Abbey. This was once thought to be the first mention in writing of Hanwell. More recent research has suggested that this, and another 'Hanwell' charter, dated from 1066, are medieval forgeries, dating from around AD 1100. It was not uncommon for ecclesiastical authorities to forge charters at this time, since, in a turbulent age, the more ancient the claim to land, the more secure it was. Certainly, at the beginning of the twelfth century, with a disputed succession between Henry I and his elder brother Robert, the Church had cause for concern.

The first definite mention of the manor of Hanwell, or Hannewelle, was in the Domesday Book, commissioned by William I, the Conquerer, in 1086. The lord of the manor was the Abbot of Westminster Abbey. At the time of Edward the Confessor (1042-1066) the manor had been worth £7; but by 1086 this had dropped to 110 shillings, or £5 10 shillings. Possibly depredations from the Conqueror's followers may have caused this fall in value. The manor was composed of eight hides and five carucates of land. Over half of this was held by the lord of the manor. This consisted of four hides and one virgate, and came with one plough. There were four ploughs belonging to the villeins (or peasants). One villein held two hides; clearly he was a more substantial man than his fellows. Four villeins held one hide, six bordars held three virgates. Other villagers, apart from these landholders were four cottagers, and, lowest of all, two serfs. There was also a mill valued at two shillings and twopence, a wood for fifty pigs and meadowland sufficient for one plough team.

Some words of explanation of the above terms should be given. It should be noted that under the Feudal system, land was held, not owned; all land was owned by the King as landlord in chief and he parcelled it out to his principal followers, who, in their turn, passed on land to be held by their tenants, all down the scale. A hide of land measured between 60-180 acres, depending on soil quality. It contained about four virgates, though this number was variable. A virgate was thirty acres. Of the ranks of villager mentioned, villeins were unfree tenants who had to work for the lord of the manor, though they were above the rank of serf, or slave. Bordars and cottars held land but also had to perform labour services to the lord of the manor.

Unfortunately, the fact that Norwood was not a parish in its own right, but merely a division of Hayes, meant that there was no separate Domesday entry for Norwood. This is a pity because a great deal of valuable information is denied to us. Unlike Hanwell, the lord of the manor was the Archbishop of Canterbury.

It is not known when St Mary's church, Hanwell, was first established. A priest was not mentioned as resident in Hanwell at the time of Domesday. Probably preachers were sent from elsewhere to instil the word of God into the populace. It is probable that the church was built in the twelfth century, though this may have been on the site of an older Saxon church. It was in this century that the first priest, Henry of Bayeux, is recorded in a document dated 1187. He was also rector of Greenford. Henry was probably either Norman or French, as were many of the priests in Norman England. The church had authority over the chapel in New Brentford when the latter was built in the later twelfth century. In order to support itself, the church was granted over eight acres of land.

St Mary's church, Norwood, which lies almost on the southern border of the parish, probably originates from Norman times, too. Strictly speaking, it was a chapel of ease for Hayes and was not officially the parish church in its own right until 1859 (Hayes church was the parish church proper, and the Rector there had authority over the church and the clergyman at Norwood). The present structure, which has been altered many times over the centuries, does contain traces of Norman and later medieval architecture. The semi-circular west arch and the responds in the north arcade are twelfth century. Henry Chichele, Archbishop of Canterbury from 1414-1444, gave money to help rebuild parts of the church, principally the chancel. He was the first and probably only archbishop to show any interest in this little church.

Although the manor of Hanwell was apparently independent at the time of Domesday, during the later Middle Ages it was combined with the manor of Greenford. Thus, the manor courts held at Greenford made the decisions for Hanwell as well. Hanwell continued to be the subsidiary of Greenford until the eighteenth century. However, by the seventeenth century at the

Knight's helm and sword, interior of St Mary's church, Norwood.

latest, local government in Hanwell was controlled by Hanwell parish vestry. There was no manor house in Hanwell. Modern road names such as Manor Court Road or Golden Manor have no connection with any ancient manor house.

We know very little of everyday life in Hanwell of this time. Almost certainly, the main preoccupation of the men of working age would have been agriculture. Wheat may have been the main crop that the peasants tilled. Given the relatively primitive tools and methods at their disposal, most of their produce was probably consumed locally. It is thought that Hanwell's agriculture was similar to that of Greenford; the two were part of the same manor, after all, and they included crops such as wheat, barley and rye. Stock raised included sheep, cows, bullocks and pigs.

A mill is mentioned in the Domesday survey, though this may have been in New Brentford, not Hanwell proper. However, in the middle of the thirteenth century, the Abbot of Westminster, as lord of the manor, built a mill here. It was probably erected in a field later named Mill Hill Field, which stood on the west side of Cuckoo Lane (now Greenford Avenue), on the crest of the hill. The mill did not have a long life – a later medieval abbot had it removed.

Hanwell's population was tiny by modern standards, though neighbouring parishes were also sparsely populated (Northolt's population may only have numbered about ninety in 1086). The Domesday survey lists seventeen men, which, assuming average family sizes of five, would result in a population of eighty-five, and this includes New Brentford, too. During Edward III's reign, Hanwell (excluding New Brentford) mustered fourteen men in response to a military assessment. If this represents the total number of able-bodied men, the population of Hanwell would still have been under one hundred.

The most important and ancient of Hanwell's charities is Hobbayne's charity. William Hobbayne owned land in Hanwell, though little is known about him personally. He may not even have lived in Hanwell. According to a court roll of 1484, he gave a house and twenty-four acres of land, then valued at six pounds, in his will to be used for 'godly uses', or charitable purposes. What actually happened with these funds will be explored in later chapters.

Similarly, little is known of Norwood in the Middle Ages, because, just as Hanwell and Greenford were linked, so too were Hayes and Norwood. It would appear, though, that, by the fourteenth century at the latest, Norwood was made of three separate hamlets; Southall, Northcote and Norwood. There was also a settlement at Dormoteswell, or Dormer's Wells.

As with Hanwell, the major activity of the populace was agriculture. Southall East Field was mentioned in 1367, but there are no other references to farming. Mills, however, are recorded. The Domesday survey lists a mill as being in Hayes, but this is probably a reference to one in Norwood. Nothing more is heard of this mill until the late sixteenth century, but there was a mill in Southall by 1433. The manorial tenants of Hayes had to perform various

Map of Hanwell in 1086, as imagined by Sir Montagu Sharpe in 1924. Its accuracy is questionable.

services to their lord; these included haymaking, harvesting and sheep rearing, and, as Norwood was part of the manor of Hayes, we can be sure that the residents there were involved in such activities.

Life in Norwood and Hanwell was peaceful as far as we know. The only known violence was recorded in 1382, when one John Braynt was attacked by seven unknown assailants and received sword wounds to his stomach. Change, though, had been very slow by modern standards. These communities were still small, agrarian societies, possibly with little contact with the outside world. Fortunately, there is more evidence for more recent history, and the story of the next five hundred years is far fuller from that of the previous millennium. However, by the end of the fifteenth century, Hanwell and Norwood had grown from small Saxon settlements into established villages, each with its own church.

CHAPTER 2
The Tudor and Stuart Age, 1485-1714

Nationally, these two centuries saw a number of revolutions – religious as well as political – and, finally, the emergence of Britain as the Protestant Great Power on the periphery of Europe. Some of these major events were echoed locally, some were not. This chapter concentrates on local developments, too, and also on some local people who emerge as individuals, rather than, as in the Middle Ages, mere names.

Perhaps the most important local development lay in the emergence of the vestries of Norwood and Hanwell as the real rulers of their localities. This followed national trends. Increasingly the manor was of less importance and was more an institution only for the conveying of land. The Tudors placed local administration into the hands of the Justices of the Peace at county level and into the hands of the parish vestries at parish level, which were supervised by the former. The actual rulers of the parish were the members of the vestry, made up of the clergyman and the substantial members of the parish; in Norwood's case in the later seventeenth century, they included representatives from the most important families, the Merricks and the Awsiters. Although Norwood was a mere subdivision of Hayes, by 1640 at least, it seems to have been a parish in all but name, administering its local affairs by itself. It certainly had all the usual parish officials, including churchwardens, overseers of the poor, and two constables, and, more unusually, two ale conners, or tasters, too (the last do not seem to have been appointed after 1809). Constables and ale tasters were appointed by the manorial court leet of Hayes.

During 1650, there was a Parliamentary survey of Middlesex. The commissioners noted that James Chibbald, minister of Norwood, received a £48 annual salary from Thomas Jennings, Rector of Hayes, though the tithes which the latter received from land in Norwood amounted to £200 per annum. They concluded that, 'we... think it very convenient that Norwood, being distinct in all duties and parish business from Haies aforesaid, should be made a parish church of itself.' They also suggested that New Brentford should be made a parish independent from Hanwell. Although the commissioners' suggestions were not accepted, it may be no coincidence that, from 1654, Norwood began to deal with its own poor, as laid down by the provisions of the Old Poor Law as codified by the 1601 Act. This meant that the parish could raise money by means of

Norwood parish chest, home of parish documents.

rates, to pay for the care of its own poor. The poor usually meant those too old, too young or too sick to work. Payments were of two main kinds; those to native parishioners, which were usually a certain set amount per week or month, and were administered by the overseers of the poor. In the 1650s, eight widows were each given monthly payments of four or six shillings. Then there were those occasional payments made by the churchwardens, to strangers who were passing through the parish and who were thought worthy of one-off assistance. These included, in 1690, 'a poor Irish woman lodgings all night… one shilling'. Pregnant women and lame soldiers were thought to be fit objects of such public largesse, too. Payments were usually between one penny (for sailors in 1712, for example) and one shilling. Those strangers caught begging, though, usually received short shrift.

The resident poor were assisted by private charity as well as public largesse. Hobbayne's charity has already been mentioned in chapter one. The income from his property was to be given to the deserving poor at the discretion of the charity's trustees and the parish officers. For example, in 1682, widow Huchin, who tended to widow Roan in the latter's last days, was recompensed with money for expenditure on coal, bread, ale, bacon and butter, to the total value of four shillings and six pence. Mr Chadd, who claimed he was suffering from smallpox, received ten shillings from the charity in 1700. There was also a poorhouse, paid for out of these funds. Some money was to be used for the upkeep of the church. In 1648, the charity paid £4 for the recasting of Hanwell's church bell. (in 1707, another £2 was paid for similar purposes).

Many charities were begun in this period by the prominent residents of Norwood, including the lords of the manor. Robert Cheseman, of more anon, gave money to twelve poor women. Francis Awsiter, in his will, dated 1625, left money for poor widows who attended an annual Good Friday sermon. Francis Courtney, by his will of 1706, gave property, whose income was to pay for the education of the children of the local poor. And there were others.

Important changes occurred to the holding of the manors in the sixteenth century. Norwood and Southall were manors belonging to the Archbishops of Canterbury. In 1543 Henry VIII received these manors from the Archbishop, Thomas Cranmer, in exchange for lands in Kent. Robert Cheseman bought these lands and became the first lord of the manors to actually reside there. Cheseman (1485-1547) was a royal courtier. His father Edward (died 1509) had been Cofferer to Henry VIII's father, Henry VII, having served him in the latter stages of the civil wars known to history as the Wars of the Roses. The Chesemans probably resided here because Windsor, London and Hampton Court, the centres of royal government, were all within easy reach.

Robert was a man of some importance, though this should not be exaggerated. He was one of 120 esquires sent to meet Anne of Cleves (Henry VIII's fourth wife – soon divorced) on her arrival to England from Dusseldorf to marry the King. He was also involved in the trials of Cardinal Thomas Wosley and Katherine Howard (Henry's fifth and penultimate wife, who was beheaded). Locally, he served on royal commissions and was a Justice of the Peace. Cheseman had his portrait painted by the great Hans Holbein.

Robert, who died in 1547, the same year as his royal master, left the manors of both Norwood and Southall to his daughter, Anne. Robert also bequeathed to Anne a certain cuppe 'with the spowte', a family heirloom, possibly. Until Anne was eighteen, Robert's widow, Alice, was to have possession of Dorman's Wells House, though the latter was allowed to stay there thereafter. Anne married Francis Chamberlayne, and their son sold the house to Lord Dacre in 1578. By the end of the sixteenth century, it was in the hands of the Awsiters, who were significant landowners (in 1649, Francis Awsiter was the biggest landowner in Norwood, with 425 acres, and Christopher Merrick was second with 241).

As in Medieval times, farming was the working lot of most of the people in these villages. Again, relatively little is known about farming in this period. There were about ten estates in Hanwell by the middle of the seventeenth century. These were fairly small; between twenty and fifty acres. Park Farm was larger, at eighty acres. Hanwell Common was used by those less well-off to gather fuel and to graze their cattle and sheep. However, according to a dispute in Star Chamber in 1613, it suffered from animal overcrowding.

Agricultural land in Norwood was, by the late sixteenth century, principally divided into four large fields. These were South Field, North Field, East Field and Middle Field, all of between 118-229 acres, and they existed until the early nineteenth century. In the sixteenth century, wheat was grown at Northcott and the villagers were allowed to graze their sheep and cattle on the common. In the following century, peas and beans were also grown and sheep grazed. There was a mill in the hamlets of both Norwood and Northcott in the seventeenth century.

There seems to have been relatively little trade or industry in either parish until the late seventeenth century, and then only in Norwood.
Brick-making was brought to Norwood in 1697 by Robert Browne, a London tiler and bricklayer. He bought land in South Field, as well as in Hayes. Brick-making in Norwood continued until the early twentieth century.

The other main commercial development was the granting of a market charter by William III to Francis Merrick (nephew and heir to Christopher Merrick) of Southall in 1698. By now, Merrick was the major local landowner, eclipsing the Awsiters. The Merricks lived in Southall Haw, a house later known as Southall Park, just south of the Oxford Road. Merrick's house is commonly, though incorrectly, referred to as Shepherd's Haw (I am grateful to Mr Ted Crouchman for pointing out that Shepherd's Haw was further to the west, along the Oxford Road, just before the junction with South Road). The charter permitted the holding of a Wednesday cattle market each week and two fairs annually. Apart from cattle, horses and grain could be exchanged.

There were two significant manor houses in Norwood. The first, which no longer exists, was the manor house at Dorman's Wells. Its demolition date is unclear. While it does not appear in Ogilby's map of 1678, its existence is hinted at in a document of 1677. In the early sixteenth century, this had been the property of Robert Cheseman. It was clearly a substantial building, for in his will, Cheseman refers to the great hall, a chapel and to the orchards and presumably fishponds which contained deer, fish and pigeons. When it passed to the Dacres, they built an enclosed park around the house. There was also a private chapel in the house. The other manor house, which was built slightly later, and which, amazingly, still survives, is Southall Manor House on Southall Green. This was rebuilt in about 1587 by Richard Awsiter.

Population growth remained slow. Between 1580 and 1589, only forty-seven people were baptized in Hanwell, and between 1680-1689, seventy-four, but death rates had risen from twenty-one in the 1580s to ninety-one in the 1680s Norwood's population, too, was slow growing. In the 1680s, 116 were baptised and 173 buried. The Revd Lysons in the 1790s, recorded that one local man, Thomas Colston, was remarkable for his longevity; dying in 1679 aged allegedly ninety-five years old. Many of those buried locally may have been non-residents.

Yet there was some increase. According to a survey of 1547, there had been only fifty-three 'houseling' people in Hanwell (indicating a total population of 265). However, by the later seventeenth century, there were seventy-three households in Hanwell, suggesting a population of around 365.

By means of maps and other sources, we have a far clearer picture of what Hanwell and Norwood looked like in these centuries, although the picture is still less than complete. Norden's map, published in 1593, shows that Dorman's Wells was a significant estate, just north of the Oxford Road, to the west of Hanwell. The settlements of Norcot and Southolde lay to the south of the Oxford Road, with Nortwoode to the south-east of Southolde. Nortcott and Southall were composed of at least thirty-three houses and seven cottages, all to the south of the Oxford Road, by the late 1590s. There were fifty-three dwellings in 1657. In 1664, Norwood contained ninety-three houses. Most of these were small; sixty-seven only possessed one, two, or three hearths. Christopher Merrick, though, lived in a house with fourteen hearths, but the biggest property, one with eighteen hearths, was the one owned by Lord Stamwell Morland.

There were four inns in Norwood by 1657, no doubt in part catering for the passing trade on the Oxford Road. These probably included The Red Lion, which still exists. Another pub which dates from this era, in the hamlet of Norwood, was The Plough. However, justice sometimes cast a jaundiced eye on the activities in pubs. In May 1656, the licence of Thomas Reddinge, of Norwood, was suppressed, 'for keeping a disorderly

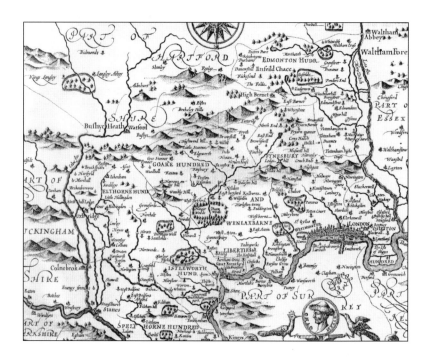

Extract from Norden's map of 1590, showing Middlesex.

alehouse'. Lest this be taken as an example of 'Puritanism' in the Commonwealth, during the early years of the reign of 'The Merry Monarch', in 1668, John Asher, a Norwood victualler, had his license suppressed for exactly the same reason as Reddinge had. Both Republican and Royalist justices, who were in most cases the same men, were concerned for the maintenance of public order and morality (the two were seen as synonymous).

Wills of the better-off in Hanwell give interesting domestic detail. Edward Millett (the elder), gentleman of Hanwell, who died in 1687, may have been a veteran of the recent civil wars, since his possessions included an old musket and pike. His property included a brew house, a milk house and several barns. In the barns there were agricultural impedimenta; carts, a plough, horses and other stores; hay, beans, wheat, rye and oats. There were also animals; eighteen sheep, three cows, two hogs and poultry. Inside his house was the maid's room, as well as the servants' room. The house seems to have been furnished to a degree of luxury. In the bedchamber were a featherbed, in the parlour, a carpet, though the hall was adorned in a more sober manner. There were three leather chairs, two tables, two cupboards, a clock and two bibles.

Religious dissent was punished. Before the Toleration Act of 1689, not attending Anglican worship was an offence. Daniel Knowling, a Hanwell tallow chandler, was found guilty on 25 March 1612, of 'not going to church, chapel or any usual place of Common Prayer on the said day nor during the six months next following.' John and Susan Gates of Hanwell were also indicted for a similar offence in 1643.

As tension between Charles I and Parliament increased, the latter decided to discover the numbers and whereabouts of Catholics in England (Charles I was thought to be sympathetic to Catholicism, and the Catholics were believed to be the arch-enemies of England, conspiring with foreign powers to overthrow the Protestant state). The parish officers were asked to make the necessary investigations in their parishes. The only Catholic in Norwood in 1640 was one Richard Cooke, a youth who had attended school abroad and whose parentage was unknown. There were no Catholics recorded in Hanwell. As the parish officials in the latter stated, 'Wee whose names are underwritten doe testifie that wee have no popish Recusantes, Men, women wives or servants inhabitinge abidinge or lodging in our towne of Hanwell.' It might be added that the constable and the churchwardens of Hanwell were all literate. There were also Protestation returns, where adult male Protestants had to be recorded, but the list for Hanwell was incomplete.

It would seem that neither the civil wars of the 1640s, nor the Great Plague of 1665-1666 had much direct local impact. The fighting at

Brentford in 1642 did not spill over into Hanwell or Norwood. There are no references to any soldiers or others being married to local girls or being buried here during wartime, and only two people (both children, from the same family) died from the plague in Norwood in 1666. However, in 1636, with a lesser plague in London, Hanwell was ordered to pay twenty shillings and Norwood ten shillings per week, in order to help relieve victims.

Yet, if these parishes escaped the worst of these mid-seventeenth century calamities, they could not entirely avoid their effects. It may be no coincidence that the plague in London corresponded to two socially important ceremonies occurring in Norwood in 1666. Susanna Damaris, daughter of Sir Samuel Morland was baptized and Johanna Maynard, daughter of the senior barrister, Serjeant Maynard, was married to John Lee

Disbursements by Norwood churchwardens, 1708.

in this year. William Leybourne, mathematician, astronomer and author, moved to Northcote in 1666, possibly to escape from the plague, too.

Hanwell seems to have been imposed upon by the Roundheads, who may not have been too unpopular locally. During the civil wars, some of the money yielded from Hobbayne's charity lands was ordered to be used for the maintenance of 'the Lord General's Army' (i.e. for the Roundheads). Robert Harris of Hanwell was appointed to a body to be consulted by Parliament on religious policy. In 1647, Lord Say, a leading Parliamentary officer, resided at Hanwell, where he returned after the great review of troops at Hounslow Heath. Another Parliamentary general, Sir William Waller who resided at Osterley Park, owned property in Norwood.

After the Civil War, it would certainly seem that Hanwell accommodated itself towards the Cromwellian Republic. On 17 October 1653, the Council of State (which had replaced the Monarchy) declared that they had received a petition from 'the well disposed inhabitants of Hanwell'. This stated that the order to invest Abraham Page as vicar should be revoked, and that Mr Nye and Mr Knight should decide whether he or William Flye should be made vicar. Flye actually served as minister of Norwood from 1658-1672, clearly no zealot as he served both Roundhead and Royalist masters.

A year later, the vicar of Hanwell was in danger of being ordered to give a larger allowance to the Minister of the chapel of New Brentford, Mr Goddin. The people of Hanwell troubled the council again in about 1656. Apparently they had been without a rector for three months. The petition desired that one Samuel Tomlins (1633-1700) of Trinity College, Cambridge, be their rector. Henry Hodges and John Lidgould, the churchwardens, and fourteen others signed the petition, stating that they had 'good experience of his fitness.' A certificate of character by Thomas Harrison and Sidney Simpson stated that Tomlins was 'able, orthodox, pious and well affected.' The latter two words are significant, in a world where political and religious loyalty were expected to go hand in hand.

One of the local losers in this period was Jonas Cooke, Rector of Hanwell, who lost his living, presumably due to his Royalist leanings, by 1644. However, Richard Sprigge, the new rector, who enjoyed an annual income of £100 from his glebe land, gave Cooke an annual allowance of £18. This was generous, as John Bennett, incumbent of St Lawrence's, New Brentford, (Hanwell's daughter church), was in receipt of a further £18 from Sprigge. A later rector, Roger Rogerson, was very zealous in protecting his finances. In 1714 he successfully sued Christopher Clitheroe, lord of the manor of New Burston (later called Boston Manor), for non-payment of the tithes to which he as rector was entitled.

Henry Hodges, Justice of the Peace and resident in a substantial house in Hanwell (in 1674, his house had fifteen hearths – a mansion indeed), who was probably the son of the Hodges mentioned above, dabbled in

political controversy. Possibly, like his fellow Hanwellians of the 1640s and '50s, he was a zealous Protestant. In about 1681, he was accused of supporting the exclusionists against James, Duke of York. Many suspected that James, Charles II's brother, and the next in line for the succession, planned to reintroduce Catholicism and to bring about arbitrary rule (Charles I was accused of similar intentions). Hodges, acting in his judicial capacity, had caused the homes of supporters of the late Charles I, to be searched, terming them, 'as dangerous as papists'. Hodges expressed joy at Oates' accusation against the Queen (in 1678, Titus Oates had invented stories that there was a Catholic conspiracy aimed at murdering the King, known as the Popish Plot). When James went abroad, he hoped that he would stay there and that all the Catholics would follow his example. He accused James of planning to murder the leader of the Exclusionist cause, the Earl of Shaftesbury. Hodges was also a republican, saying that 'a Commonwealth was the best government for this nation.'

Despite their best efforts, the schemes of Henry Hodges and his confederates were defeated and James became King in 1685. At first, Norwood Vestry showed their support towards him. His Coronation was celebrated locally, the church's bellringers being paid seven shillings and sixpence for ringing 'on the Coronation of our Soverigne Lord and King James the Second'. A 'Book of Thanks for the Victory over ye Enemies' was purchased by the Vestry. The 'enemies' were Monmouth's Protestant rebels who had been smashed at Sedgemoor in 1685.

National events were reflected in other payments made to the church bellringers. The bells were routinely rung for royal anniversaries, such as the King's birthday and the anniversary of his Coronation. November the fifth was also celebrated by bellringing, and the ringers were given refreshment in return for their labours. For example, in Norwood, on 5 November 1693, they received a leg of pork, bread and drink, costing the parish eleven shillings. Fifth November was also a celebration of Protestantism's triumph over Catholicism; as well as Guy Fawkes' abortive plot, after 1688, it marked the arrival of William of Orange in England, which led to the abdication of the Catholic James II (1685-1688).

William's accession was welcomed, and his rule (1689-1702) celebrated. William was often absent from England, at war with James' supporters in Ireland or against his French allies on the continent, and William's safe return to England was marked by bellringing. British victories over the French during the War of Spanish Succession (1702-1713) were also celebrated. The Duke of Marlborough's victory over the French at Blenheim in 1704 was marked by the parish bells being rung at the cost of three shillings and sixpence. With the end of the war, the vestry paid small sums (four or five pence each) to wounded soldiers passing through the district on their way home – in 1710, fourteen were thus aided.

Several misdemeanours were recorded as happening in the Hanwell and Norwood of these times. These were dealt with, as was all crime in the county, by the Justices of the Peace at the Middlesex Quarter Sessions Court, though lesser offences were dealt with at Brentford Petty Sessions. Most of it was relatively minor, but there was a murder in Hanwell in 1588. Agnes East of Hanwell, had, on 15 January, between eight and nine o'clock, been struck on the head with an axe, while at the hall of Thomas Millet's house. The killer was one John Pryor, who subsequently fled and we hear no more of him; such were the difficulties of enforcing the law. Another violent assault, though with a happier outcome for justice, was when Richard Weekes and Thomas Simpson, both from London, attacked Thomas Kidwell on the road in Southall. Kidwell was robbed of £46 9s 6d. The Court found, on 8 September, 1595, that both were guilty and Simpson was executed.

Punishment, when it did occur, was very public. On 25 April 1609, the following sentence was passed on one Henry Porter:

> He shall be whipte at a cart's tayle thurrough Norcott street twoe severall dayes the next weeke, vizt on Tuesdaye and Thursedaie next between the hours of x [ten] and xi [eleven] in the forenoon, to be performed by the constables, for drawinge of Mr Merrick's coache into the myre, and the fowlinge it verye loathsomely within with clowts.

Possibly Porter was dealt with so rigorously because Merrick was a JP himself. Twice (in 1675 and 1678) Norwood constables had to whip men (probably vagrants) before sending them away.

Monument to Christopher Merrick, St Mary's church, Norwood.

St Mary's church, Norwood, early eighteenth century.

There were several thefts in 1617, so that John Goryn, a Norwood tailor, gave securities for John Hedges, a Norwood labourer, in order to answer for Hedges' being abroad at night, 'when divers robberies have been committed'. In 1636, one William Scudamore was accused of breaking into John Allenson's house and stealing jewellery, though he claimed he was innocent. Edmund Lawrence of Fulham was robbed of £15 'neer Brent Bridge towards Southall' in 1658.

Apart from strictly criminal offences, the JPs dealt with other matters. A common one was dealing with recalcitrant fathers or parishes as regards bastard offspring. On 10 October 1610, for instance, Edward Allen, miller of Norcott, was ordered to pay for the maintenance of his bastard child. Deserted wives had to be supported. Alice Heather, born in Greenford, had lived in Norwood for nine years. She married an Ealing man, who left her and so Norwood parish had to provide for her. Sometimes the gentry disagreed with the parish officials. In 1645, Richard Awsiter, gentleman of Norwood, was accused by the churchwardens of conveying away a manservant of his who had made a fellow servant pregnant, thus placing the burden for the baby's upkeep on the parish, not the father.

Dealing with troublesome alehouses was another hardy perennial. On 26 March 1608, Edward Welder, yeoman, and Ann, his wife, were asked to answer for 'their contempts in victualling without a licence.' In 1697, Thomas Atkins, victualler of Southall, was ordered to have his licence suppressed because his alehouse was said to be 'ill-governed'. Short measures or indifferent beer was the crime committed by John Watson, Southall yeoman, in 1608. Petty offences included cheating during gambling. Anthony and Edward Trappes were on the run in 1617 for cheating £9 5s from Edward Ruddinge at false play. Anthony Trappes was later charged. This catalogue of crime may seem immense for two small parishes, but it must be remembered that they were spread over almost two centuries.

By 1714, Hanwell and Norwood were far less dependent on the manorial courts than they had been in the Middle Ages, and were now virtually self-governing, by means of the parish vestries. Much remained the same; they were agricultural in character and their populations had not grown significantly. They had taken note of national events and in some cases had been affected by them, albeit in a relatively minor fashion.

CHAPTER 3

The Hanoverian Age, 1714-1837

The reigns of the first four Georges and William IV saw more peaceful changes in England than the previous two centuries. Canals and railways began to transform the landscape, and these will be considered in the next chapter. Industry and agriculture began to undergo great changes, too, though the former was not particularly noticeable in Hanwell or Norwood at this time. Developments were generally slow and steady, rather than dramatic. The beginnings of education for both poor and rich, religious tolerance and the more humane care of the mentally ill were also important aspects of this era.

By the late eighteenth century, the old administrative link between Greenford and Hanwell was severed, except that the manor courts were still held together. Their only function was to register changes in the holding of land. For example, on 14 October 1745, it was noted that John Mares, a customary tenant had died. He had held three acres of land from the manor. His next of kin was Anne Harding, the widow of his cousin, and she was duly admitted by the court as tenant. The position of lord of the manor was more about social status and local prestige than anything else. One important later lord of the manor was George Villiers, Earl of Jersey who owned Osterley Park, just over Norwood's borders (though he rarely resided there). He was lord of the manors of Norwood and Southall from 1806-1833. The Jerseys owned much land in Norwood and Hanwell.

Another severance of old connections was the separation of St Mary's church, Hanwell and St Lawrence's, New Brentford. In 1747, the Hanwell rector gave up his rights to the tithes of New Brentford, which meant that the minister of St Lawrence's was independent as he now posessed his own income.

The Hanwell Vestry was busy in dealing with the problem of the poor. For example, John Law, who was out of work, had his allowance raised from two to three shillings a week, but was told to find work soon. The widow Heard was forbidden her allowance for the Vestry found her to be a 'notorious drunkard and prostitute'. The cost of poor relief was rising; in 1776, the annual cost was £128, in 1813-1814, £550. Although there was no workhouse, houses were rented at no or low cost to the poor, and pensions were given to the elderly. After 1834 the poor were no longer the responsibility of the parish; the passing of the New Poor Law in 1834 saw to that – unions of parishes combined to build workhouses and relief

was administered internally. The Vestry also had to deal with smallpox and rabies. In 1785, they agreed to pay for inhabitants to be inoculated against the former, while mad dogs were to be immediately destroyed.

Norwood had similar problems. Following national trends, the cost of poor relief rose, being £252 in 1777 and peaking at £850 in 1821 (hardly surprising given the slump following the end of the Napoleonic wars). The local response was to build a workhouse, in 1814, which was near what is now Featherstone Road. But it was not the Bastille-like structure of popular imagination; there were only twelve inmates in 1803 and eight in 1834. As with Hanwell, after 1834, the poor were transferred to the workhouse in Uxbridge.

Two intriguing references in the Norwood churchwarden's accounts for 1744 and 1745 were payments given, apparently, to anonymous slaves, sixpence to two in 1744 and one shilling to seven in 1745. Presumably these were black men. The mystery is why slaves should be in receipt of poor relief. If they were runaways it would be unlikely that they would seek help from officialdom, if they were not, it was their master's responsibility to feed them, and parish officials were not usually known for their generosity. It is probable that these men may have been discharged sailors, after all the Thames at Brentford was not far away, and to the parish officials, all black men were slaves.

Steps were also taken to deal with local crime. In 1787, a ten-foot cage was built at the entrance to Church Field. This was to hold suspects prior to an examination by the Justice. By 1821, crime was thought to be such a problem that an association was formed in Hanwell to offer rewards for anyone who helped catch and convict murderers and thieves.

There were improvements in road transport in the eighteenth century. In 1714, the Uxbridge Turnpike Trust was founded, which set up toll gates to charge road users in order to pay for repairs of the road. Toll gates were set up at Hanwell amongst other places en route. Although there had been stage coaches from London to Oxford in the seventeenth century, it is not certain that they travelled along the Oxford Road through Hanwell and Norwood. They certainly did so in the eighteenth century.

Coaches took two days to travel from London to Oxford. In 1742, the coach would leave London at seven in the morning and reach Oxford at five on the following afternoon. Travel by horseback was quicker – though rather saddle-weary – taking only one day. Later in the century, the coaches were faster; mail coaches travelled night and day, whereas most others only travelled in the daytime. During the period from 1790-1810, these coaches stopped at Southall on their runs from London to the Midlands and Wales. According to Pigot's Directory of 1826, Southall's roads were very busy, 'It is a place of considerable thoroughfare; coaches and carriers to Oxford, Birmingham, and other parts… passing through here almost hourly.'

Although stage coaches have a romantic image, accidents did happen, as they do with any form of transport. In August 1835, the Worcester coach known as The Telegraph, was going through Hanwell towards the bridge and crashed, because the front axel broke. The coachman and some of the passengers were injured, and other passengers decided not to preceed with their journey. One man, however, waited for another coach and proceeded with his journey to Worcester.

Stage coaches were the least uncomfortable and fastest form of passenger transport available on land, excepting horses. Inns such as The Coach and Horses in Hanwell and The Red Lion in Norwood served as stops on the long journey. They also catered for long-term visitors, too. According to the directory mentioned above, 'It [Norwood] is a place much resorted to in the summer time and good accommodation may be obtained at the inns.'

Bridges often needed repairs: in 1774, £27 was spent on the bridge linking Hanwell and Greenford, but attention was needed again in 1832. This was especially serious because a manservant of the Revd Archdeacon Potts had drowned while attempting to cross the bridge. One possible reason for its dilapidated state was that there was some doubt about whose responsibility it was, the parishes themselves, or of the Bishop of London as lord of the manor. Usually the parish had had to do the work or be indicted by the county Quarter Sessions. Certainly, Edward Levick, carpenter of Hanwell, had been repairing the bridge for over fifty years. Eventually, a compromise was reached and both bishop and parish paid £100 towards the work.

In the late eighteenth century, the successive incumbents of St Mary's Hanwell, were a father and son, the Reverends Samuel (1737-1812) and George Glasse (1761-1809). Both were socially well connected, classical

Old Bridge across the Brent at Hanwell, near Greenford.

Hermitage, north side, Hanwell.

scholars and active in parish affairs. Samuel was rector from 1780-1785 and was a chaplain to George III. He was described as 'a popular and eloquent preacher'. He also took a large part in the rebuilding of the church. The old church, which had stood there since the Middle Ages, was demolished and a new structure had been put in its place in 1782. The old church had been too small for the increasing population, which had doubled between 1757 and 1782. The new church was designed by Thomas Hardwick, a New Brentford mason, and was a whitewashed brick and slate building.

After Samuel Glasse resigned in favour of his son, he remained active as a county Justice and still attended Vestry meetings. His son George, chaplain to the Duke of Cambridge, replaced him as rector and published a large number of sermons and other works. Glasse the younger seems to have been learned and witty, but was indiscreet and lacked prudence. Despite his wealth, or perhaps because of it, he was fond of gambling, ran into money troubles and hanged himself at The Bull and Mouth inn, London, in 1809.

Religious matters in Norwood were less dramatic. At the beginning of the nineteenth century the Curate resided locally, though he was also non-resident vicar of Grandborough in Buckinghamshire. There were two services on Sunday, including a sermon in the morning. Holy Communion, though, was administered less regularly; only four times a year at the major Festivals, where between thirty and forty people took bread and wine. However, as in Hanwell, there was insufficient accommodation in the church for the increasing number of parishioners, but unlike Hanwell, attempts to remedy the situation, in this case by trying to increase the number of pews or to erect a gallery, failed. In 1824 there was a plan to demolish the old church and to build a new one, but three years later, the

St Mary's Hanwell, 1800.

Hanwell Parish church and rectory, 1806.

plan, for some unknown reason, was scrapped. On a more positive note, the first organ was installed in 1830, and was situated in the gallery at the back of the church (until 1892).

Although Protestant nonconformity was legal by 1689 and Roman Catholicism by 1791, there were few signs of anyone of either persuasion here until the early nineteenth century. The Revd Anthony Hinton, Curate of St Mary's, Norwood, claimed, in about 1809 that 'There are as in most parishes some few Methodists but they have no place of meeting here and I think their No. rather decreases'. This was not so in Hanwell. In 1818, a meeting house of Independents was registered at a house near to The King's Arms. Another one was founded in 1821, though only one was listed by 1831. Both founded schools, too.

During the Jacobite rebellions in 1715 and 1745, parish constables had to make lists of local Catholics. Catholics were suspected of being sympathetic to these rebellions which aimed to restore the Catholic Stuart monarchy in the shape of the Old Pretender, the son of the deposed James II. However, Catholicism was first noted in any numbers in Norwood at the beginning of the nineteenth century. Dr John Collins, a Catholic priest, kept a school for boys at Southall Park, from at least 1809 until the 1830s. There was, as yet, no Catholic presence in Hanwell.

The maps made in the eighteenth century show far more local detail than those of earlier centuries. The John Rocque maps of the mid century are particularly useful. Apart from the Oxford Road, the two other main roads in Hanwell are those branching to the north and to the south of it. To the south is Boston Lane, leading to New Brentford. To the north is Snapes Lane, which branched off northwards into Cuckoo Lane, which went towards Greenford.

There were three main settlements in Hanwell. The first was that on the Oxford Road, which was almost wholly to the north of the road, and between Snapes Lane to the west. The second gathering of dwellings was that on the top of Snapes Lane. To the east of this settlement lay Hanwell's great house – Hanwell Park, the property of Charles Gosling, which contained extensive grounds, and bordered the southern part of Cuckoo Lane. Finally, at Church End, which was that road leading west from the north end of Snapes Lane, was St Mary's church and several other buildings on the spur of the hill, overlooking the River Brent.

The eastern part of Norwood was sparsely populated, though there were many roads intersecting with the Oxford Road. To the south was Wind Mill Lane, presumably so called because of the windmill there. To the north of this road, forming a cross roads with the Oxford Road was Water Mill Lane. This ran past the pond, Dorman's Well; the building marked on the map of the time may represent a mill. The old manor house does not appear, though the orchard which was in its grounds is indicated. Further westwards on the Oxford Road, was Dorman Lane, running northwards. There is another bridge crossing the Brent to the south of Hanwell Bridge, called Billets Heart Bridge, and the trackway leading from it joins Windmill Lane.

The only property, apart from the mills in this eastern part of Norwood was a property called Cheassey Chace, which lay to the south of the main road, not too far from the bridge. The main settlements are further to the west and south west. To the west is Southall, with houses on both sides of the road, and a few on an unnamed road to the north. Waxley Farm lies to the north west of the Oxford Road. To the south west of Cheassey Chase are the church and and a few other buildings in Norwood. According to Brewer in 1816, these were 'Houses constructed on the borders of the Green. On this agreeable spot is a considerable neighbourhood of respectable villas, nearly all of which are of an ornamental character, and many possess extensive and finely cultivated tracts of garden land.' There was also a cluster of buildings on the road running south of Southall towards Norwood.

The number of houses steadily increased. In 1793, Lysons noted that there were 107 in Hanwell, but there were 164 in 1837. In Norwood precinct in 1793 there were 129 in total. Of these, forty were in the hamlet of Norwood, thirty-three a little further to the north-west, on Southall Green, and the rest – fifty-six – were on or near to the Oxford Road, in what was now termed, 'Norcott alias Southall'. In the memoirs of the Revd Benjamin Armstrong, who came to Norwood in 1830 as a youth of thirteen, this district is rightly described as rural. Armstrong related the story:

> It was thought advisable… to take some small place in the country for the benefit of our health… He [Armstrong's father] took a very pretty and rather commodious cottage-residence at Southall Green, Middlesex, about a mile out of the high road to Uxbridge and exactly 10 miles from Tyburn Gate… Having been long pent up in town, Annie and myself viewed Southall as a second Paradise.

Similar praise was bestowed on Hanwell. An article in *The Gentleman's Magazine* in 1800, went into rhapsodies about the views around the church: 'After passing the door of Mr Glasse's hospitable dwelling, a scene bursts upon the view which few spots in the environs of the metropolis can vie with. A serpentine walk, kept in the most perfect order, leads from the house to the bottom of a steep descent, where a rustic temple terminates it'. In 1826, it was

Old Rectory, Norwood Green.

described, more prosaically, as a 'small and respectable village… The situation of this village is very pleasant, and the air is considered exceedingly pure'.

Although there were a number of gentry residing in Norwood and Hanwell (in 1832 they numbered ten and twenty-six respectively, including professional men and clergymen), the two localities cannot be described as having aristocratic pretensions, as Acton and Ealing did in the eighteenth century. As the 1832 directory modestly phrased it, 'several families of distinction, sensible of these advantages [fresh air], have fixed their residence here'. It was, after all, convenient for London and for country pursuits. However, on 7 June 1806, four royal dukes attended the baptism of the Revd Glasse's son at St Mary's Hanwell, with the Duke of Cambridge (whose chaplain he was) acting as godfather.

Agriculture, as it had always done, dominated these two rural parishes. The significant change was enclosure. Much of Cuckoo Hill was enclosed at the end of the eighteenth century. In Hanwell, enclosure was first mooted in 1792, but it was not until years later that action was forthcoming. Much of Hanwell Common (which was located in the eastern part of the parish) was enclosed by an Act of Parliament in 1816, concentrating land in the hands of fewer owners. This Act enclosed 350 acres of common fields, and had been done at the instigation of George Villiers, Earl of Jersey, and other landowners. As some form of compensation, the Commissioners appointed to survey the land were to allot four acres to the parish who were to use it for the benefit of the poor (whose actual rights to use the common land had been legally tenuous anyway).

Prior to Enclosure, the system of crop rotation was practiced in Norwood's open fields. Some land was left empty, or fallow, and the crops grown elsewhere were wheat, barley or oats and clover. In 1797, in a report to the Board of Agriculture, John Middleton reported that, 'much of the soil of Norwood is most highly productive loam, possessing that happy medium of texture which fits it alike for the production of corn, pulses and roots and its staple is five or six feet in depth on a bed of gravel.' According to the first official census in 1801, of the 697 Norwood residents, 220 were involved in agriculture; a very high percentage indeed.

Eight large open fields, amounting to 1,000 acres in Norwood, were enclosed under the Hayes Enclosure Act of 1809, the work of surveying and arranging for this to be put into effect took time, and was not completed until 1814. Most of this land belonged to the Earl of Jersey; in all, he owned 966 acres of land in the precinct (the descendant of a previous lord of the manor, Robert Awsiter, by now owned but fifty-eight acres). Wheat, beans and peas were grown after Enclosure. By 1821, there were only four farms in Norwood, cultivating a total of 679 acres.

There was little industry – apart from the brick-fields – established locally, and according to the 1801 census, only thirty-three people in Norwood were employed in 'trade, manufacture and handicraft'. It was said of Norwood in 1832 that 'it possesses no particular trade'. John Nash, architect and builder, who supplied bricks for Buckingham Palace, was licensed by the Earl of Jersey to dig brickearth on his land in East Field in 1826. There was, however, a vitriol factory that was established by 1816, owned by Henry Dobbs, or Dodds as his name was sometimes spelt. This was located in Heston, on the south bank of the Grand Junction Canal, though Dobbs resided in Norwood. According to Brewer, in his *Beauties of England and Wales*, the factory was run 'on scientific principles, and of producing, in consequence, very superior vitriol, and other articles connected with that trade'. In Hanwell, there was even less industry, except for a glove workshop which was founded by John Fownes giving employment to poor women and children in 1795.

The cattle market continued to prosper, remaining in the hands of the Merrick family until the early nineteenth century. William Welch bought the lease and built a market place in 1805, which occupied three acres of land just to the south of the Oxford Road. Ten years later, it was said that this market was second only to Smithfield for the sale of fatted cattle.

Each parish possessed a few shops which supplied basic goods. In Southall in 1826, there were two blacksmiths and a saddler to help attend to agricultural needs. For other needs, there were two boot makers, a butcher, a baker, a tailor and a grocer. Hanwell possessed rather more shops; twenty-six in total. Among them were a dress and corset maker, two bricklayers, and a furniture shop. There were also two resident surgeons.

There were eight inns in Norwood in 1821. Apart from their obvious function, some also served as meeting places for friendly societies which, in return for small regular payments, the poor could, in times of hardship receive some benefits. In 1803 there was a benefit society of forty-eight members in Norwood. The Union Society was another, and this one was registered in 1830 as having its meeting place at The Red Lion. The White Hart, Southall, being on the Oxford Road, was a convenient meeting point and functioned, *inter alia*, as a post office, by 1826.

As ever, the population continued to rise slowly. The number of births had increased; in Norwood, this went from 134 in the 1730s to 208 in the first half of the 1790s, which appears impressive. However, deaths rose, too, from 148 in the 1730s to 224 in the first half of the 1790s. For Hanwell, the picture was similar. Even allowing for the probability that most of the baptisms were of local children and that some of the burials were those of strangers, the rise is not notable. The Revd Lysons recounts an amusing incident from the Hanwell baptism register, which he termed a 'Singular mistake': 'Thomas, son (daughter) of Thomas Messenger and

Elizabeth his wife, was born and baptized, Oct. 24, 1731, by the midwife, at the font, called a boy, and named by the godfather, Thomas, but proved a girl.'

From 1801, with the inception of the national census, we have, at last, reliable figures. In 1801, there were 817 people in Hanwell, and 1,213 in 1831. Norwood's population grew from 697 in 1801 to being 1,320 in 1831. Some of the latter growth was due to the increasing birth rate and the decreasing death rate, as recorded in the parish registers. The number of baptisms in Norwood in 1800, 1810, 1820 and 1830 respectively were, thirty, nineteen, forty-four, thirty-eight, and those for burials were twenty, twenty-three, thirty-one, seventeen; a pointer to an overall rise as the former outnumbered the latter.

We know little about the recreations of the people at this time. In Hanwell, there was an agricultural contest recorded in 1787, to see who could plough in the straightest manner. Lads played cards on the Heath in 1813, much to the Vestry's disapproval. Charles Burton records the enthusiastic celebrations of 5 November 1833, but noted that the use of wood for the bonfire would deprive many of warmth in the coming winter. John Yeoman, writing at the end of the eighteenth century, records cricket being played between the men of Southall and Ealing. For the better off, there was racing and field sports. Armstrong records a great deal of this activity near Norwood in the 1830s. As a fifteen-year-old, he remembered:

> Having heard that Mr De Burgh's stag hounds met at Sipson, I repaired thither on my pony and found a brilliant field assembled of above 200 scarlet coats, among whom were the Dukes of Cumberland and Wellington and Sir F. Burdett. I was delighted and

View of Hanwell, from a late eighteenth-century painting.

*View of Hanwell,
looking east from
Norwood, 1795.*

amazed at this brilliant display, and my pony bolted at the onset, nor
stopped till he and his rider were completely knocked up.

Pheasant shooting at Osterley Park was another pastime of the local gentry.
The cult of Sensibility was a dominant feature of later eighteenth-century
Britain. It manifested itself in concern by the middling sort of people for
the less privileged. Such movements included anti-slavery societies,
prison reform groups and the creation of foundling homes for orphans.
Predominant in these movements were men such as William Wilberforce,
John Howard and Jonas Hanway. Such concerns were evident in
Norwood and Hanwell, as shall be noted below, and Hanway himself was
connected with Hanwell.

For much of his early life, Hanway (1712-1786), had travelled in
Persia, an unusual destination for eighteenth-century English travellers.
On his return to England, he wrote a book of his travels, and then
devoted his life to good works, especially where children were concerned.
Hanway was a friend of the Revd Samuel Glasse, and often visited the
parish. It was here that he was buried. It should be noted that Hanway was
also somewhat of a crank. Apart from his attempts to popularise the umbrella,
he was anti-Semitic, opposed women sea bathers and was against the drinking
of tea as being effeminate – noting that the Englishmen who defeated the
French at Agincourt had not been tea drinkers.

Schools began to appear in this district during the long reign of George III.
The first was the Elisha Biscoe School. Biscoe, (1705-1776) was the steward
to the lord of the manor of Norwood and Southall, from 1750, and a rich
man in his own right. In 1767, he laid aside a sum of £3,500 to pay for a
school for the children of poor parents. This stood on Tentelow Lane,
Norwood Green and existed until 1950. Children entering the school were
to be nominated by a list of gentlemen chosen by Biscoe and their successors.

The aim of the school was for a schoolmaster and his wife or housekeeper to instruct thirty-four boys and six girls of poor parents who lived in Heston, Hayes or Norwood. The boys were to be taught reading, writing, accounts and arithmetic, but, above all, in the 'Principles of the Christian Religion'. As for the girls, they were to be taught reading and writing, too, but also more feminine domestic subjects; including knitting and 'house business' in order that they might make good servants or wives.

Children were to begin at school between the ages of eight and thirteen and not remain after fifteen years of age. On leaving school, each child was to be given a bible. Attendance at church on Sunday was compulsory. School hours were 7 a.m. to 5 p.m. in summer and 8 a.m. to 4 p.m. in the winter. The schoolmaster and his wife were to receive an annual salary of £40.

Biscoe's son, also called Elisha, took up the running of the school after his father died, as instructed in his will. However, by the 1820s, there were discrepancies in the running of the school, especially where the accounts were concerned. This occured because the trustees who were supposed to be in control had never met. However, by 1826, matters were running on a more acceptable footing, with records and accounts being properly made and kept.

In Hanwell, the Hobbayne charity was used to found a school for local children in 1781. The charity had previously sent children to schools in neighbouring parishes. In 1781, the trustees decided to contribute £30 per year to establish and maintain a parish school. They were assisted in their endeavours by the Revd Samuel Glasse, who

Elisha Biscoe School,
Tentelow Lane,
Norwood.

Jonas Hanway, 1712-1786.

bought a house to be used as a school by the church . As with Biscoe's school, the number of pupils was small; twenty-four initially, rising to thirty in 1790, and possibly a few fee-paying pupils, too. Apart from the charity money, public subscriptions also helped to support the school. A gale destroyed the school in 1800, but it was rebuilt by the younger Glasse, then re-housed in 1807. By 1817, the school was expanded and opened to more local poor children.

There were other schools in Hanwell and Norwood in this period. In Norwood, in 1833, there were 151 pupils (in addition to those attending the Biscoe school). Perhaps the most well-known school in Hanwell was the Hanwell Collegiate Academy, founded by the Revd James Emerton in about 1830. This was a private boarding school for about sixty boys, and was designed to prepare pupils for Sandhurst or for the Indian Service. One pupil was Charles Burton, and his diary of events there, though it makes for dull reading, gives a good impression about the daily routine at the school. Apart from subjects such as French, Mathematics and History, there were lots of prayers, playing cricket and drawing.

One noted Hanwell teacher was John Diamond (1731-1807). He made his living by teaching others to read. There seems nothing very remarkable about that, except that he had been blind from the age of one month. Apparently his memory compensated somewhat for his blindness, and his pupils had to have some preliminary knowledge of their letters. He also had his writings published, in particular, in 1790, he published accounts of the solar eclipses of 1791-1793.

Perhaps the one institution which put Hanwell on the map in the nineteenth century was the County Asylum, built in 1829-1831. Although it was located in the parish of Norwood, it was known as the County Asylum at Hanwell, since it was physically nearer the settlement at Hanwell, though within Norwood's boundaries. Its presence was to cause much annoyance to many in Hanwell, (the association of a parish with an asylum for the insane was hardly an appealing one, and of more of this in chapter five), but it did an immense amount of good work for its inmates.

Following an Act of Parliament in 1828 (this was the decade of Liberal Toryism), enabling counties to build and maintain county lunatic asylums at public expense, the Middlesex justices took the initiative. However, they also wanted to limit expenditure, with the result that the premises, when built, were too small, even though they cost £124,440 to build. Dr (later Sir – he was the first psychiatric doctor to be knighted) William Charles Ellis (1780-1839) was appointed as Superintendent of the asylum and his wife was Matron. Ellis, who had been in charge of an asylum at Wakefield, already had many ideas about the treatment of the insane. Principally, he believed in the therapeutic

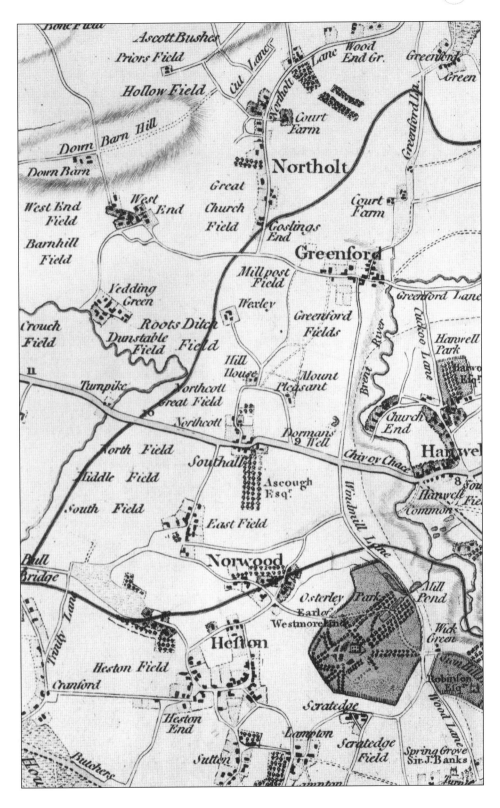

Extract from Cary's map of Middlesex, 1800.

aspect of work. Inmates should not just be guarded but be encouraged to take part in manual work, in order to help rehabilitate them for life in the outside world. For the male patients this was usually gardening, for the female, needlework. The inmates also baked enough bread for their own needs. These were not new ideas; the Quakers of York had written about such matters in 1785, but it was a major step forward in putting such ideas into practice.

At first, there were about 600 patients, but the number grew. In 1836, the weekly cost per inmate was six shillings and five pence. Ellis was fortunate in knowing the right people, too. He had good contacts at court and in due time the Adelaide Fund was established, named after the Queen. People were invited to subscribe to set up a fund to help inmates who were declared sane enough to venture into the outside world, and needed money to establish themselves in work.

National events had a greater tendency to intrude into local life. Polling during general elections often occured at Brentford and it is probable that in 1768, when the radical John Wilkes was trying to secure his election to the Commons, there was a great deal of excitement in and around town. This probably spilt over into Hanwell too, since Hanwell Common was the last staging post of the crowds en route to the poll. It should be remembered that eighteenth-century elections involved much eating, drinking and general rowdiness. Indeed, Norwood constables received payment for their attending the polls. In 1784, the Revd Glasse, the sole Hanwell voter, cast his lot on Wilkes and William Mainwaring, the Tory candidates, who won (Wilkes had mellowed with age). In Norwood and Southall the handful of electors preferred George Byng, the losing Whig candidate. In 1802, the tiny electorate of Norwood and Southall swung towards Mainwaring instead (who lost).

Towards the end of the eighteenth and the beginning of the nineteenth centuries, the greatest danger facing Britain was that posed by the mighty French military machine, led by General Napoleon Bonaparte. Despite the superiority of the Royal Navy, the danger of invasion was thought to be very real. The Revd George Glasse of Hanwell preached against the French menace, and, more practically, helped to form an armed force against them.

In 1803, Glasse, having taken upon himself the office of superintendent, from which he had to later withdraw, had handbills distributed through the parish inviting interested parties to attend a special meeting of the Vestry. Many of the parishioners responded positively, agreeing to form a local corps of Volunteers, to be allied to similar corps of Heston and Norwood. Other parishioners, especially ladies, promised to contribute money to pay for uniforms. Eventually, thirty-eight Hanwell men joined fellow patriots of Heston, Norwood, Southall and Northolt. The men drilled in the grounds of Hanwell Park. Although there was no invasion, and, even if there had been, the military value of these men would probably have been minimal, their activity did show that here, as elsewhere in the country, there was a practical spirit of opposition to the French.

The accounts of St Mary's, Norwood, for December 1805, record the victory at Trafalgar; 'Pd for a form of Prayer, postage, etc., for a General Thanksgiving for the Great victory obtained by the Ever to be lamented Lord Nelson. Four shillings, eleven pence.' With the French navy sunk, Englishmen could sleep safely and many could forget all about the wars – there is no reference to any local celebrations for Waterloo in 1815, for instance.

Norwood and Hanwell were still small agricultural villages in Middlesex at the eve of Queen Victoria's long and illustrious reign. Yet, as we have seen, they had not been static during the long eighteenth century. The emergence of local schools, the building of the asylum, the reign of the enlightened Ellis there, and the first, though as yet puny, emergence of trade and industry in Norwood are all of some significance. Two of the most important developments have not been mentioned yet – the coming of the canals and the railways, and these will be examined in the next chapter.

CHAPTER 4
Canals and Railways, 1790s-1990s

As Hanwell and Norwood were only a few miles (seven and nine, respectively) to the west of London, they could not escape being permanently marked by the transport revolution which was both caused by and stimulated the expansion in commerce and industry which was to make Britain the workshop of the world. This chapter looks at the building of the canals and railways and their impact on the society and economy of these two parishes which they passed through. Unlike some, the author does not think that they alone transformed these two villages into suburbs; but they did make that transformation possible. It also discusses two railway accidents which took place near Southall. However, this chapter has deliberately avoided any in-depth discussion of the railway stations or Brunel's local masterpieces; the Wharncliffe Viaduct and Windmill Bridge (The Three Bridges), for these will be detailed in the guide notes for the walking tour after chapter eight.

Industrial output was rising in eighteenth-century Britain, but the inadequate state of transport threatened to inhibit the expansion of markets for such goods as were being made, mainly in the north of England and the Midlands. London and the south of England were a huge potential market. What was needed was an easy, quick and reliable method of transporting goods from Birmingham to London, and, as water transportation had always been the best method, canals seemed to provide the answer. After all, a horse-drawn barge could pull a fifty ton load, whereas horse and cart could only manage 300 pounds in weight.

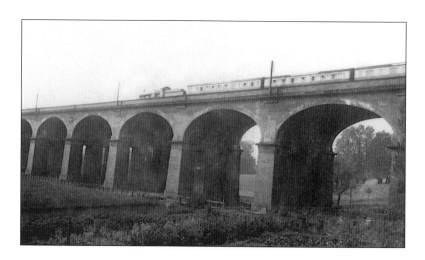

Wharncliffe Viaduct, Hanwell, c. 1900.

Grand Junction Canal, looking north, with St Bernard's Hospital in background.

The Duke of Bridgewater had had a canal opened near Manchester in 1761 and others followed in the pioneer's footsteps. In 1793 the Grand Junction Canal Company received the royal assent for their plan to link Birmingham via Braunston, Northamptonshire, with the Thames at Brentford, a route of ninety miles. By 1798 the canal had been cut as far as Uxbridge. It was completed by 1805. The canal passed through Norwood from west to east and joined the Brent to go south to Brentford, along part of the west and south boundaries of Hanwell. Traffic began to use it from 1800.

The connection to the Thames was not really ideal for attracting much of London's huge trade. So it was also decided in 1794 that, in order to take goods nearer London than the Thames at Brentford, a Paddington arm, from Bull's Bridge in the south western portion of Norwood, to the village outside London called Paddington, should be cut. There were no locks on this route, thus quickening the journey. This canal went northwards from Norwood, along its western boundary and through Northolt, Greenford and other parishes on its way eastwards. After years of wrangling, the work began in 1799 and was finished by 1801. There was a grand opening ceremony. Horses pulled two gaily decorated barges from Paddington to Bull's Bridge. This journey took three hours.

London acted as a magnet. It attracted raw materials, such as bricks (London was expanding at an immense rate at this time) and returned manufactured goods and rubbish, such as brick-field debris. Much of this rubbish was being recycled in the countryside. Some barges were specialised. Clayton's tar boats had holds for liquid cargoes, and so were able to remove crude tar for distillation from Southall Gasworks, which used coal and oil for making gas. The tonnage which was received at Paddington was immense. In 1810 the annual incoming tonnage was 113,200, outgoing 67,728.

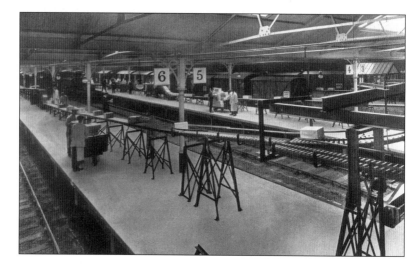

Gravity conveyor to GWR goods station, Maypole Margarine Works, Southall, 1925.

There were two establishments in Norwood which particularly benefited from the canals, both having their own docks. One was the asylum, where the goods made by the inmates could be removed by boat. The second was the Otto Monsted Margarine Works, of which more will be heard in chapter five. This factory's dock was called the Maypole Dock. It opened in 1913 and it dealt with a large tonnage of coconut, oil, grain, fish, cheese and margarine. In 1914, there was 55,000 tons of traffic, in 1920, 84,500, but in 1928, the year before the factory's closure, only 30,000. The canal branch which had to be cut here was half a mile long, and lined with concrete, unlike earlier canals. It cost £27,670. Some brick-fields in Norwood and Hayes had their own private canal branches for ease of transporting bricks.

The canal seems to have been at the peak of its profitability in the 1830s; toll receipts stood at £184,311 in 1834-1836, but fell thereafter (in 1870-1872, the figure was two thirds lower than it had been in the 1830s). This was partly due to the railways, which were able to capture the passenger market, not that that had ever been very significant anyway. More importantly, perishable goods travelled faster by train, which did mean a noticeable decline in canal usage. Yet the canals carried on their trade into the twentieth century. The tonnage passing through Top Locks in 1914 was 440,516, but by 1928 it was 391,006.

The effects of the canal on Southall's economy were significant. As noted in chapter two, brick-making had begun in Norwood in 1697. The digging of the canal would have revealed, if it were not known already, that the soil, which was clay, could be turned into bricks. By 1894, there were four large brick-fields, all of which were sited near to the canal, and three of these almost next to the Paddington branch. One had made a special cut from the main canal to the middle of the brick-field. Others had their own docks. Leases for land to be used as brick-fields often included a clause about the proprietors being allowed to make their own cut and dock to link up with the canal. The canal's competitor, the railway, did not compete in the transportation of bricks to London, probably because the short distance involved made such a proposition uneconomic. Dr Hounsell concludes, 'It is difficult to imagine a major brick-making industry operating in West Middlesex without the presence of the canal.' Without the canal, local brick-making would have probably remained on a small scale. Furthermore, the presence of the brick makers would have created extra demand for the goods of local shopkeepers and publicans, too.

The canal also assisted the railway. Parts of trains and lines were brought by canal. Nearly all the timber used for sleepers was unloaded and treated at Bull's Bridge. However, once the Brentford Line had been built, railway supplies could be more conveniently transported by this line without having to rely on the canals which were now thought to be less useful. It is probably not coincidental either, that the steam flour mill and the oil, gas and vitriol works in Southall were all either next to the canal or had the benefit of a canal branch. However, the overall local economic impact should not be exaggerated; after all there was no such industry in Hanwell. As the Pigot's Directory of 1839 observed of Southall, 'It possesses no particular trade'.

The short-term social effect of the canal building was to bring labourers into Hanwell in order to cut the canal. Apparently, 'the position of the publicans was a trying one, requiring much attention when the workmen were served'. The Vestry, though, were pleased with the way that the publicans sold their wares. However, their stay does not seem to have been permanent and, having done their allotted tasks, they moved elsewhere for work. Another effect was that between 1802 and 1830, eight people are recorded in the burial register as having drowned in the canal, presumably after drinking in the local pubs. The canal was a pleasant place for children to fish, according to Benjamin Armstrong.

In 1929, the Grand Junction Canal Company merged with other canal companies operating around London to form the Grand Union Canal. The canals were nationalized in 1948. After nationalization, a British Waterways Repair Yard was established at Bull's Bridge. There were also boat-building facilities, dry docks and slipways here. By the 1960s, however, canal trade was still in decline, due to competition of railway and road. It became more and more for purely recreational use.

Railways began in the 1820s. Unlike canals, which were built to satisfy an existing industrial demand, they were largely speculative, hoping to be able to cater for a demand that was yet to be created. In 1832, a line was proposed to be built from London to Bristol, but this was turned down. A

year later, the Great Western Railway was formed, and employed the services of a young engineer, Isambard Kingdom Brunel, who surveyed the proposed route. He decided to run the line along the Thames Valley in order that it would be as flat a route as possible, thus saving expense by building the minimum number of tunnels and viaducts.

The company gained royal assent in 1835 and work soon began. In 1837, Brunel prepared a specification for a contract between Hanwell and Acton. George Henry Gibbs, who was involved in the work, kept a diary about events during the construction. He was often concerned about what he saw occurring. In October 1837 he was 'alarmed at the continual subsidence of the embankment at Hanwell'. Four months later, the embankment was not completed, but he still believed that the work would be finished by the end of March. However, ten more men had to be assigned to work on the Hanwell sections in September 1838. This was especially important as the through service was now running. The first section, from Paddington to Maidenhead was opened on 3 May 1838, and passenger services soon began thereafter. Initially there was only one station between these two termini, but others were soon opened. These included Hanwell on 1 December 1838 and Southall on 1 May 1839. The railway ran through the northern part of Hanwell, north of the Uxbridge Road, but ran through the southern part of Norwood parish, far south of that road.

At the beginning, the frequency of the railway service was minimal. In 1839, trains stopped at Hanwell on their way to Paddington four times a day, at 8 a.m., 11 a.m., 3 p.m. and 7 p.m. From Hanwell, they travelled westwards to Slough and Maidenhead four times daily, too, leaving at 9.30 a.m., 1.30 p.m., 4.30 p.m. and 8.30 p.m. Services did improve; by 1849, there were eight daily trains instead of four, but only one catered for third-class passengers.

By 1880, there were thirty-eight trains every day running between Southall and Paddington, and the number grew; in 1900 there were forty-five, in 1910, sixty-five. The First World War inevitably reduced this frequency, but in the 1930s the number had reached sixty-three. The Second World War and its aftermath reduced the frequency to fifty by 1960, and in 1971, trains were only hourly; a great reduction indeed. The distance from Hanwell to Paddington is seven miles and in 1971 the hourly trip took sixteen minutes, at a weekly cost of £1 5s 10d. By the 1990s, trains were every half hour, but there was no Sunday service.

Initially, fares were relatively high. In 1839, there were no third class tickets, first class returns cost two shillings and sixpence, with second class one and nine pence. Prices fell, and by 1906 they were at their lowest; two shillings for a first class return, one shilling and four for a second return and one shilling for a return third class. However, by 1960, prices had returned to their 1839 level, and have continued to rise ever since.

Hanwell railway station.

Hanwell and Elthorne railway station, 1969.

Goods traffic as well as passengers used Southall station. One large local user was the gasworks. Coal and coke were supplied by train from Yorkshire and Derbyshire. From around 1895, the gasworks had its own railway sidings. Quaker Oats' factory at Southall also used the canal for transportation of goods. However, goods traffic at Southall station had virtually come to an end in 1965, though Shell Mex and BP had fuel sidings there in 1967. Probably increased competition from road haulage companies led to this decline.

Another railway branch line, one of the last of Brunel's creations (he died in 1859), ran from the Brentford Docks on the Thames to Southall, a distance of about four miles. It opened for goods in 1859 and for passengers in 1860. Originally there were a dozen trains each way per day, and from 1880, there were sixteen. In 1904 a new station was built en route to serve Osterley Park and Wyke Green, called Trumper's Halt, after

Southall railway station, looking west, c. 1950.

a local landowner. This new station helped increase business, serving as it did the Wyke Green Golf Course and the residential outskirts of the expanding western Hanwell, and the number of trains running rose to thirty-five each day. It was closed as a wartime economy measure from 1915-1920. When normal passenger services were restored, due to local pressure, they were at a reduced rate. Trumper's Crossing was closed in 1926 and in latter years the service was not frequently used, but it continued to be in service until 1942. Despite a proposal in 1954 that this service be resumed, it came to nothing. The freight service continued until at least the 1960s, though. The volume of goods traffic it handled was considerable; in 1860 it was 58,000 tons, in 1956 it was 180,054.

Another branch line was built connecting Southall to Victoria, via Addison Road, Kensington, opened in May 1863. For the first twelve years, there were eight or nine daily trains, but by 1896 this number had been cut back to four. Following a revision of the service in the following year, the number of trains increased. However, in 1915, because of the war, all trains on this route were withdrawn and, unlike those on the Brentford branch, never restored.

The construction of the railway and the viaduct in the mid-1830s brought Irish labourers to Hanwell. There were a couple of incidents recorded. Firstly, in 1836 at The Stag inn, harsh words were exchanged between the Irish navvies and the local men. When Dr Walmsley, the rector, acting in his capacity as a Justice of the Peace, summoned the police from Brentford, he became the target for the Irishmen's wrath. Three men were convicted and were imprisoned for two months. The Railway Company were told to prevent such outbreaks in future, or else police or troops would have to be stationed at Hanwell to keep the peace.

There was another disturbance in 1838, this time at The Coach and Horses. When mounted police tried to break up the affray, they were attacked by men and women armed with shovels and pickaxe handles. Nine people were convicted and fined thirty shillings each or less. Probably, most locals, except perhaps the publicans, did not regret that their stay was a temporary one.

According to Benjamin Armstrong, the building of the railway through Southall was a catastrophe. In his memoirs, writing of 1836 when the railway first began to be built, he wrote:

> A remarkable change for the worse took place about this time in the hitherto retired neighbourhood of Southall. The railway spread dissatisfaction and immorality among the poor, the place being inundated with worthless and overpaid navigators [their daily pay was three shillings; a reasonable rate] the very appearance of the country was altered, some families left, and the rusticity of the village gave place to a London-out-of-town character. Moss-grown cottages retired before new ones with bright red tiles, picturesque hedgerows were succeeded by prim iron railings, and the village inn, once a pretty cottage with a swinging sign, is transmogrified to the "Railway Tavern" with an intimation gaudily set forth that "London porter" and other luxuries hitherto unknown to the aborigines were to be procured within.

Armstrong greatly exaggerated the case. Southall was still a relatively small place in the decades following the opening of the railway, as population figures in the next paragraph indicate. The navvies were not a permanent fixture; by 1839 most, if not all of them would have gone to seek pastures new. As to the flight of the gentry families, eleven are recorded as being in Southall in 1839, nine in 1845, including Armstrong's father. As to public morality, a directory declared, in 1839, that, 'The neighbourhood of Southall is exceedingly respectable'. In 1852 in a railway book, reference was made to 'the pleasant village of Norwood', which also suggests that the railway's 'evil' effects were limited.

It is often stated that the building of the railways resulted in the local population dramatically increasing. This does not seem to have been the case, at least not at first. The trains were too infrequent and ran too late to have much impact. Furthermore, initially the railway did not offer workmen's returns. In 1831, Hanwell's population was 1,213; in 1851, twelve years after the completion of the railway, it was 1,547. In Norwood the figures were 1,320 and 2,693 respectively. However, Norwood's population rise was largely accounted for by the building of the asylum and the subsequent arrival of over 600 pauper lunatics.

Some local historians have written nonsense about the effects of the railways. Kate McEwan in *Ealing Walkabout* writes of Southall, 'Once the level crossing opened in 1839, the first factories soon appeared'. Although there was a little industry in Southall in the mid-to late nineteenth century, this was largely the result of the canals. Rather, Paul Kirwan is more accurate to describe the coming of the railway as 'The most important *single* contribution towards the development of Southall as an industrial town' (my italics). This was, however, a gradual process. Apart from the brick works and the factories already noted, there was very little industry in Southall until towards the end of the nineteenth century, and what there was was largely due to the canals. In 1852, a railway booklet stated, 'About Southall itself, little need be said'. The main economic impact of the railway on Southall at this time was limited to the transportation of vast amounts of cattle and sheep from Somerset and elsewhere to Southall for the cattle market. However, this was not a happy development for local farmers as increased competition forced down prices. It would seem that the railway did not have a significant local economic impact until the very last years of the nineteenth century. The opening of the Otto Monsted Factory in 1895, just south of the main GWR line was a major occurrence and undoubtedly influenced by the railway, though many materials for the factory came via the canal.

However, it was only in the early twentieth century that Southall could be properly described as an industrial town. *The Official Guide to Southall and Hayes* in the early 1920s attributes its industrial growth to the excellent transport facilities, 'Commercially, no situation could be happier, offering at once a wide choice of means of transport both by rail and water to every part of England, including the great exporting centres.'

Industrial shunting locomotive at Southall gasworks, 1920s.

Flooding at the canal, a view from Trumper's Way, December 1979.

It goes on to add that, 'There are still some excellent factory sites adjacent to the railway and in other parts of the district'. AEC was based in Southall from 1927-1979 and they built rail cars, including the pioneer W1 rail car in 1933, among other vehicles, and some were tested on the Brentford branch line during the quieter moments. Yet it had taken several decades after the opening of the GWR line, and the Brentford branch too, before this transformation had come about. There were other reasons for this development, which will be explored in later chapters, and, though Kirwan is probably correct that the railways were the most important factor, they were not the only one.

The local railways had a military use in the First World War (1914-1918). Then there were great demands made on the railway service. As we have seen, passenger trains were reduced. The War Office and the Ministry of Munitions needed trains to transport troops, coal for the Royal Navy, and government stores, especially guns, ammunition and explosives. Railway stations had to be altered to cater for this additional demand. In 1915, the government paid for an additional siding and loading platform to be built for Victor Tyre Works, Southall, which cost £302. A year later, this had to be extended. Additional siding accommodation was built at Hanwell station in 1918 at a cost of £3,897.

Transport accidents are a sad fact of life; and ever since their inception in the 1820s, the railways have proved no exception. There were two fatal incidents near Southall. Both involved two trains, one of which was a fast passenger train travelling from the West Country.

The first occurred in 1847. The Exeter Express, which was travelling towards London at a fast speed, broke the tyre of one of its 7ft single driving wheels. These pieces shot out and one broken section killed two

passing drovers. The other splinters derailed a passing goods train. The express train was now about to cross the Wharncliffe Viaduct and a major disaster seemed imminent. Fortunately, the goods train was derailed away from it and the express stayed on the rails, crossed the viaduct and, having stopped for the driver to inspect it, arrived at Paddington only minus the tyre. Brunel had argued the case for a gauge of seven feet instead of the smaller and more conventional gauge, reasoning that a 7ft gauge would be safer as it would give trains greater stability, especially when travelling at speed. He seems to have been proved right.

The better-known Southall train crash occurred on Friday 19 September 1997. It was 1.15 p.m. when the Intercity train from Swansea was travelling (at 90mph) on the last few minutes of its journey to Paddington when it collided with an empty gravel train, which was traversing across the path of the other train. The main impact of the crash was taken by the second and third carriages, which were full of passengers. Manjit Singh, of Villiers Road, may have prevented another crash when he flagged down a third train which was heading for the crash scene; it stopped 100 yards away.

The situation was bad enough anyway. Superintendent Mike Smythe, in charge of Southall Police, described the scene as 'Carnage – there were dead bodies and bits of bodies across the track, thrown from the train. It was quite horrific.' In all, six people had died and 170 were injured. The emergency services and others were quick to reach the scene. Villiers school offered accommodation to some of the survivors.

There was a public enquiry in 1999 as to why the accident occurred and to apportion blame. British Rail had been privatized only a few years before by the previous government and there were some who blamed privatization for having put profit before safety. Others claimed that fault lay with the way the privatization was handled; breaking up the British Rail monopoly into many different parts meant that confusion and uncertainty reigned, and that this was to blame.

The train was equipped with the AWS (Automatic Warning System), which had been first introduced in the 1960s. Apparently, according to train driver Larry Harrison, the AWS system had not been in operation when he left Swansea. He had reported this at the time, but to little apparent effect. There was also some question as to whether Harrison himself was to blame. Allegedly, he had both feet up on the dashboard when the crash happened and he did admit partial responsibility for the tragedy.

There was a move to prosecute Great West Trains for corporate manslaughter. Although the company was fined £1.5 million, this did not occur. Indeed, the whole affair ended somewhat inconclusively. The newer ATP protection system which was to be introduced on the trains was scrapped in favour of a cheaper option, though doubt was expressed as to whether the former was foolproof.

On a lighter note, trains and canals have given many people a great deal of innocent pleasure. The GWR Preservation Society, the canal enthusiasts, and the ubiquitous 'heritage industry' hold regular events which celebrate the transport achievements of the past. That this area is particularly suitable for such events may lie in the fact that there is so much transport history still existing; such as the Wharncliffe Viaduct, Top Locks and the Windmill Bridge (Three Bridges). This interest has certainly had some happy effects. The retention of Hanwell station's Victorian character was protected after local pressure on British Rail in the 1970s. Unfortunately the elaborate roof decoration of Southall station was removed in the 1960s, before such local interest was particularly strong. For rail fans, such architectural ornamentation is still visible at Slough station, however.

The Grand Junction Canal and the Great Western Railway eventually transformed the landscape which they traversed. Their impact on Hanwell and Norwood was neither as catastrophic as the likes of Armstrong feared or as revolutionary as some later writers have claimed. The canal did stimulate the already existing brick industry in Norwood, and it and the railway made possible Southall's transformation into an industrial town at the beginning of the twentieth century. Hanwell would never have become the densely populated suburb of London that it was becoming by the end of the nineteenth century without the railway. But these changes were gradual and did not happen overnight. The next chapter will discuss the major developments in these two parishes in the Victorian era, the era of the railways.

GWR Preservation Society open day, 1982.

CHAPTER 5

The Victorian Age, 1837-1901

These sixty-four years saw the transformation of Hanwell and Norwood from agricultural villages into rapidly expanding towns. The number of buildings and the size of the population rose by an unprecedented scale and necessitated that all the problems of growth be dealt with; changes in local government and the subsequent increase in their powers to build social amenities such as sewers, roads, schools and so forth. It was also a period of private lunatic asylums, as well as steady progress in the County Asylum, which, by its mere presence, began to attract local criticism. As well as secular amenities, new churches including those of non-Anglican denominations came into being.

Local government had been in the hands of parish vestries from the seventeenth century, but by the nineteenth century this form of administration was no longer thought to be sufficient for modern needs. They still existed, but became less and less important as their functions were hived off. As noted, in 1834, the old parish responsibility for the poor had been largely removed. By 1885, Hanwell, and by 1891, Southall-Norwood (as the old parish of Norwood was now known) had been formed into local boards for local government purposes, and, in 1894, both became Urban District Councils.

Hanwell fire brigade, 1896.

Hanwell Recreation Ground and St Mary's church, c. 1900.

In 1859, the old dominance of Hayes over Norwood ceased. Norwood became a parish in its own right, rather than a mere precinct. The practical impact of this was less important, for, as we have seen, Norwood already dealt with its own affairs. Yet this was the formal recognition that Norwood had grown enough to be considered independent in local affairs, both religious and secular.

It is also significant that the name of the new local government bodies for the old parish of Norwood were both pre-fixed with 'Southall-Norwood'. This recognized what had been evident for several decades at least, that the growth in the parish was chiefly in the old hamlet of Southall, both around the Uxbridge Road and on the road to its south, South Road, whereas the settlement around Norwood Green and St Mary's had remained relatively small. From now on, Southall will be used instead of Norwood when referring to the whole of the old parish.

In the late nineteenth century, there were a confusing number of local administrative bodies, including lighting inspectors, the sanitary authority and the highway board. Some of these bodies only covered part of the parish. The vestries had appointed a number of officials, but these were few in number, often amateur, receiving no remuneration except for expenses and annual dinners. These new local government bodies were very different. Firstly the members were elected. Secondly, the officials they appointed were paid professionals, such as sanitary inspectors, medical officers of health and surveyors. More was expected of them, too. In order to house them, adequate premises were needed. In Southall, a town hall was built in 1897 on the High Street; in Hanwell, Cherington House, an early nineteenth-century building in Cherington Road, was converted into offices in 1892.

What these bodies achieved may seem mundane, but they were also essential for the well-being of these two expanding towns. In Southall, there were proper gas and water works by the late 1870s, and proper drainage was laid by 1890. Both Southall and Hanwell constructed sewage works by the Brent in the 1890s. Hanwell bought land for its first public park, Churchfields Recreation Ground, which opened in 1898. A cemetery was built in Southall, as the churchyards were full.

Population growth in both Southall and Hanwell was dramatic in the later part of the nineteenth century. In 1841, Southall's population was 2,385; in 1901 it was 12,499. Hanwell's growth was equally rapid: in 1841, 1,469, and in 1901, 10,438. In both cases, the biggest percentage rise was in the 1890s. These more than five-fold rises, were far more than those for the county of Middlesex as a whole in the same period, which only doubled. In 1890 there were almost 1,000 houses in Southall. In part these growth rates were not due to indigenous factors; the arrival of the County Asylum (which had 1,005 inmates by 1841, and 2,000 by 1880), and two residential schools for the children of poor parents, the Central London District 'Cuckoo' School in Hanwell in 1856 and the St Marylebone School in Southall two years later, contributed, both having hundreds of pupils. Birth rates rose, according to the parish registers. In Hanwell, in 1837, forty-five were baptized; in 1901 it was 215. In Southall the figures were 54 and 204. These numbers, of course, refer only to those baptised in Anglican churches, but the trend is clear.

There were also people coming into Southall and Hanwell from elsewhere, and though there had always been some parishioners who were not native, their numbers probably rose, helped by better transport. These 'immigrants' were chiefly from other parts of the British Isles. However some were from Europe and a few from the Empire. Notable European immigrants to Southall included skilled personnel to manage the Otto Monsted margarine factory, and builders, the Hansons, all of whom were

Otto Monsted margarine factory, viewed from the south, c. 1900.

from Denmark. There was a Captain William Cahill of Her Majesty's Indian Army, born in the East Indies, resident in Southall High Street with his family in 1861, and there was Major General William Paske, born in Madras and late of the Bengal Army at South Lodge in 1881, but, generally speaking this was not a parish for retired Empire builders, unlike Ealing. Another exception was Henry Hitch, who briefly resided in Sussex Gardens. At Rorke's Drift, in the Zulu War of 1879, Hitch won the Victoria Cross.

In the last quarter of the nineteenth century, building in Hanwell both north and south of the Uxbridge Road, was rapid. Generally speaking, those houses to the north, especially north of the railway line and towards St Mary's church, were detached and semi-detached houses for middle-class residents, many of whom doubtless used the railway to travel to work in London. The Golden Manor estate was one such development of large houses with gardens. Some of the large estates were being broken up and the land sold off to developers. For example, Sir Montagu Sharpe (1856-1942) sold Brent Lodge and Hanwell Park; both houses were demolished for building purposes.

To the south of the Uxbridge Road, apart from those houses adjoining the road, and a few adjoining Lower Boston Road, there had been relatively little building. Towards the end of the century, the picture had altered immensely, as it had to the north of the Uxbridge Road. There had been a great deal of building to the south of the northern half of Boston Road, and roads which ran to the west of that long thoroughfare were built up, too, some almost reaching the Brent. More of the Uxbridge Road had been built on each side.

The population expansion in Hanwell between the end of the eighteenth century and the early nineteenth century, though not as large as that later in the century, did mean that in 1837, the King (William IV) was petitioned to allow an enlargement of St Mary's church. However, it was realised it was necessary to completely rebuild the structure, to make it possible to seat 750 people. In 1841 this occurred, following the design of Messrs Moffat and Scott. Thirteen years later the church was struck by lightning, and part of the steeple fell off.

In Southall, the picture of suburban expansion was similar. Old settlements expanded and new ones were created nearby. Southall's principal thoroughfare, which connected the Uxbridge Road to Norwood, had centred on Southall Green, which lay to the south of the railway station. There had been hardly any building on the northern part of this road. By 1894, this hitherto country lane had been largely built upon; with detached and semi-detached houses on the east side, and with some terraced houses on the south western side. In Southall

Brent Hill, later Lower Brentford Road, Hanwell, 1881.

Green, many new houses had been built on the western side, especially between Featherstone Road and Western Road, and between the latter and Adelaide Place.

Yet we should not exaggerate the extent to which these places had been built up. There was no building along the Uxbridge Road to the west of Southall (which centred around that road, and North and South Roads). Likewise, though the centre of Hanwell had been built up and was expanding, there was still much open land to both the north and south. As an 1892 source remarked of Southall, 'The wanderer in search of the picturesque will do well to tramp along the lanes hereabouts, for here is the country, as yet quite untouched by suburban London'.

It has been noted in chapter three that Norwood and Hanwell were thought by late eighteenth and early nineteenth-century observers, to be attractive rural districts. By the late nineteenth century, this was no longer the case. For example, Walford, in his book *Greater London*, published in 1882, is very disparaging about Hanwell. He writes,

> The Village of Hanwell mainly consists of a long and wide High Street, which carries on the line of houses from east, and ends at a bridge at the west end of the village beyond which is the county Lunatic Asylum. The houses and shops are most irregularly built and yet they are far from being tasty or elegant. In fact, a duller and plainer street is not to be found, even in Middlesex.

Yet only six years previously, Thorne, in *Environs of London* had written of Hanwell, 'The neighbourhood is green and pleasant, gently undulating, mostly pasture land'.

Both writers looked unfavourably upon Southall. Thorne thought that, 'Southall is a busy but not an attractive place. The country is flat and disfigured by extensive brickworks, though in some directions there are green fields, shady lanes and pleasant walks'. Walford stated, 'It is the centre of a very flat and dreary district'. Both approved of Norwood. For Thorne it was, 'a pleasant though flat district. There are neat cottages, many trees, the well cared for church…'. And Walford wrote that Norwood, 'consists of several handsome and substantial houses, surrounding a triangular village green of some 20 acres, adorned with fine Elms'.

In both Southall and Hanwell a number of Anglican churches were built in the Victorian era, due to the demand caused by the increasing population. In Southall, these were St John's built in 1838 and Holy Trinity opened as an iron hut in 1869, being replaced by a permanent structure in 1890. In Hanwell, St Mark's was built in 1879.

Nonconformity also gathered strength in these parishes in this period, even in Southall where it had been almost non-existent in the early nineteenth century. The Primitive Methodists and the Wesleyan Methodists both established chapels in Southall in the 1870s, on Western Road and South Road, respectively. The Baptists established a chapel on Western Road in 1889, which was rebuilt in 1901. There were also Salvation Army and Brethren operating in Southall in the 1890s. There was a Methodist chapel on Boston Road Hanwell from 1837-1869, another was built on Lower Boston Road in 1884.

Benjamin Armstrong records religious dissension breaking out in Southall in 1837. Henry Dodds, who gave money to build St John's, was a dissenter and was waging a war of words with Mr Moore, of St Mary's. He hoped to put in a Low Church minister at St John's to further his cause. There were some ferocious sermons at first; 'The heat was intense, many of the women, unused to such powerful appeals, fainted away and the majority were disgusted.' However, Armstrong went on to happily conclude that although the first two ministers of the new church were of the Low Church, they 'had too much principle to allow Mr D. to dictate to them on points of doctrine.'

Catholicism arrived in Hanwell in the later nineteenth century. Beginning with a mission at Miss Ann Rabnett's house, Clifden Lodge, it grew and so in 1864, the Church of Our Lady and St Joseph was built on the Uxbridge Road. It was not consecrated until 1918 because it had been in debt before then. There was also the Catholic Convalescent Home for women and children on the Uxbridge Road. Catholics in Southall worshiped in the tithe barn at the Manor House in the late nineteenth century.

Before the advent of compulsory secular education, the churches were busy in founding or promoting local schools. St John's church school, Southall, just off King Street, was sponsored by Henry Dodds, the vitriol

*Old St John's church,
Southall, 1901.*

*Hanwell National
School, 1855.*

manufacturer and was established by 1838. It was a small school, with a single classroom for both sexes. By 1869, there were nearly 200 pupils who had to pay a small weekly fee. In 1891 it closed. St Marylebone school has been referred to already. It was on South Road and catered for children from the parish of St Marylebone, London. There were also National and British Schools, which were funded with public money. Norwood Bridge school (founded 1862) was one, North Road school (founded 1851) was another. The latter became a Board School, which was administered and funded by the local school board, a secular body.

In Hanwell in 1843, there was the National School, for over one hundred pupils, catering for Anglicans, and in 1871 there was a British school, for the children of nonconformists. Both charged nominal fees. The rivalry between the two schools was such that the lads fought a pitched battle in 1880. Both were taken over by a non-sectarian School Board in 1900.

Hobbayne's Charity was still active in the field of education. The school was rebuilt on the corner of the Lower Boston Road in 1855. Increasing numbers of pupils, (in 1870 there were 200) led to the premises being extended on several occasions. Subsidised meals were provided in 1886.

The Central London District school, built on Cuckoo Hill (therefore known locally as the Cuckoo school) is one of the most famous local schools. One reason for this was that Charlie Chaplin and his brother attended the school in 1896-1898. The other was because of its huge size; there were 1,000 pupils there. It was built for children of poor parents who resided in central London. However, there were outbreaks of illness in its early years and many died. Emphasis was on practical skills; for employment purposes, many of the boys entering the Royal Navy, the girls becoming domestic servants. The school also prided itself on its Silver Band and on its sports teams winning prizes. It also had its own farm.

Even before the arrival of compulsory education, many local children seem to have attended school. In 1851, 208 Southall children went to school; in Hanwell the number was 242, but this included those from elsewhere who boarded at the Revd Emerton's College.

The Forster Education Act of 1870 stated that schools should be provided out of public funds where they did not exist; in 1880, schooling up to the age of ten years was made compulsory. In practice, this legislation took time to take effect. Dudley Road and Featherstone Road schools were the only two purely state schools which were established in Southall, and then, only in the 1890s. They were relatively small; the former had only three women teachers at its inception.

Central London District school, Hanwell.

There seems to have been few private schools in either Hanwell or Southall at this time. The boys' boarding school began by the Revd Emerton, Hanwell College, had folded by 1882. There was also a private girls' school from the 1840s to the 1860s. Forty-eight pupils attended the four Dame schools in the parish in 1842.

Although the advent of the railway resulted in the demise of the stagecoach, the process was a slow one. In 1845, seven years after the opening of the railway in Hanwell, four stagecoaches made regular stops there, and one was still plying the route as late as 1878. In 1872, road transport was assisted by the abolition of the toll gates in that year. Other forms of road transport developed. An omnibus left The Duke of York pub twice each day, at 8.30 a.m. and 9.30 a.m. in the 1870s and '80s. This new form of horse transport succeeded (eventually) where stage coaches had failed because they could carry far more passengers. Horse trams ran along the Uxbridge Road from 1867-1900.

Public entertainment was more common, and organized, than in earlier centuries. A cricket club was established at Hanwell in 1850, and soon, consisted of forty members. Three cricket clubs were founded in Southall. One was specifically aimed at working men and played the game on Norwood Green in the 1890s. Tennis and golf clubs were established in Southall in the same decade. A Working Men's Club and a Constitutional Club were formed in Hanwell by the 1890s.

Perhaps the most famous local club to be formed was the Hanwell Town Band, often known as the Hanwell Silver Band. This had arisen from discussions in 1891. Mr Wallis, publican of The Viaduct allowed the band to hold their weekly practice in one of his rooms. There had

Horse bus at Hanwell, c. 1890.

Hanwell Broadway,
c. 1870.

been a generous response for subscriptions for the band to purchase instruments, so, under the conductor's baton of Mr Williams, the band made its first public appearance, in Hanwell Broadway in early 1892. The first full concert occurred in the Union church in February 1893, including selections from the works of Mozart and Handel.

Both parishes were still largely agricultural for much of this period. This was more-so in Southall than Hanwell. In Southall in 1842, there were 916 farm animals; mostly sheep, but also horses, cattle and cows. In Hanwell there were only 186, and of these there were no cows. Wheat and hay were Southall's principal crops, but oats, beans, turnips, potatoes and other crops were also grown. Hanwell produced 600 tons of hay in 1842, more than Southall did, but by any other measurement, the former produced far less. However, Southall's farming was still relatively primitive, with a minimum of machinery being used, due to 'a conscientious though mistaken solicitude for the welfare of the labouring classes'. However, the soil was well manured – the latter commodity coming from London, presumably via the canal.

In Southall in 1851, farming was the most common male occupation, employing 185 men, compared to sixty-one in the brick-making trade (the second biggest local employer). In the 1860s, there were four largish farms in the parish (Dormer's Wells, Waxlow, Sparrow and Warren) and there were two in Hanwell (Park and Cuckoo). Apart from Sparrow Farm, all these were a distance from the main settlements, surrounded by fields. In the 1860s, three quarters of Southall's acreage was used for farming, mostly wheat. There were also a few market gardens in both parishes. By

1876, Thorne could still write that, 'Farming is a leading occupation' in Southall. However, these were not good times for the cattle market. The coming of the railways had meant that cattle from the West Country were being sold there and forcing prices down for the Middlesex farmers. There was also a downturn in trade, so that in 1869 it was no longer a cattle market, but a general market. Yet, despite competition from the London markets, cattle were still sold there.

Farming, though, was on the decline by the end of the nineteenth century. According to the census of 1871, only ninety-six men were employed in agriculture in Southall, a significant fall from 185 in 1851, especially as the overall population had risen in those twenty years from 2,693 to 5,882.

Industrial development was evident in Norwood, though not at a vast rate. There were the brick-fields, mostly to the west of the main settlements, as noted in chapter four. Perhaps more important was the establishment of the Otto Monsted margarine factory and, on a more artistic note, the arrival of the Martin brothers in 1877, with their pottery works. There was also Norwood Flour Mill, on the banks of the canal. It converted to using steam power, but ceased in about 1900. Another large enterprise was Brentford Gasworks, which was relocated next to the railway in 1869.

Otto Monsted, a Dane, had a vast margarine factory built in Southall, just south of the railway line, in 1893-1894. He had an existing plant at Godley, Cheshire, but needed room to expand his operations. Southall seemed an ideal place. His new factory was the largest such factory at the time anywhere in Europe. It officially opened in 1895. By the standards of the time it was a model factory, with high standards of cleanliness. In 1895, there were 200 employees, and the managing director until 1910 was Mr E.V. Schou, another Dane, as were the technical staff.

Workers at Otto Monsted factory, c. 1900.

Martinware Wally Birds, 1890s.

Walter Fraser Martin, potter, by kiln, Southall, c. 1890.

The Martin Brothers moved to Southall from Fulham in 1877. There were four brothers in total, Robert, Charles, Edwin and Walter. They set up their pottery works in a disused soap factory on the canal bank at the end of Havelock Road. They produced their salt-glazed pottery there for the next four decades. Many of their works are 'grotesques'; the ugly pair of Wally Birds are a case in point. However, they never became rich and often their works had to be used to pay their bills.

Although it was men who ran the major enterprises just mentioned, women often ran smaller concerns. For example, in Southall in 1839, of the six public houses, two – The King of Prussia and The Wolf – were run by women. Mary Brown ran a carpenter's business. The children at Biscoes' school were taught by Mary Ann Vincent as well as by John Vincent (presumably her husband).

Martinware fireplace,
now located at
Pitshanger Manor, Ealing.

Of course, it is a far cry from this to talk about equality or emancipation.

Industries in Hanwell were very few. The best known one was the violin factory of W.E. Hill and Sons, which originated in the eighteenth century. William Ebworth Hill (1817-1895) moved to Hanwell from Brentford in 1890 and lived at Heath Lodge. One workshop was set up in the back garden and another at York Place. On Hill's death, his son Alfred continued the business, which expanded in 1900. A skilled workforce repaired old violins and made violin accessories.

In 1839 the County Asylum had its most famous physician. This was Dr John Conolly (1794-1866), an Irishman from Birmingham. He was the first man in England to end the old practice of placing restraints on inmates. Conolly was only superintendent of the asylum until 1844, but he remained as visiting physician for several years, while, like Ellis, he went into private practice. He lived in Lawn House, a large house in its own grounds, situated on the north side of the Uxbridge Road in Hanwell.

For the patients, life was busy. According to the report for 1843, 110 attended in-house school classes. They were also industrious in making aprons, shoes, caps, gowns, sheets and other simple garments. The garden produce they helped create made a profit that year of £2,500. Patients involved in such work were given extra beer and tea as a reward for their work. Their diet was generally monotonous; oatmeal and bread for breakfast, soup and stew for dinner and bread and cheese for supper. Beer was the usual beverage. The asylum even had its own brewery.

It was not universally popular locally. Although the asylum was in Southall, it was known, incorrectly, but very definitely, as the Hanwell Asylum. So much so in fact, that there was a movement to rename

The Lawn, home of
Dr Conolly.

Brent Lodge, Hanwell, c. 1890.

Hanwell. One possible name suggested by the Revd Emerton was Bishop's Town. Another suggestion was Elthorne, which was the name of the ancient Hundred (a sub-division of the county, further divided into parishes) of which Hanwell had been part. Although the railway station was renamed Hanwell and Elthorne, these other proposals came to nothing, but Coney Hatch, a parish in northern Middlesex in which another public asylum was built, was renamed New Southgate.

There were several private asylums in Norwood and Hanwell for those inmates whose relatives could pay fees (the County asylum largely catered for the poor, whose treatment and accommodation were paid for out of the rates). Both Ellis and Conolly ran private asylums. The asylum at Southall Park was run by Dr Robert Boyd, and had on average eighteen patients. They came to a tragic end in 1883, when it was destroyed by fire, which killed Boyd, his son and four patients. There were also asylums at Vine Cottage, Featherstone Hall and The Shrubbery.

Apart from the Martin Brothers and Dr Conolly, there were few other residents of note in Victorian times. Those few included Dr Thomas Hume who had been physician to the Duke of Wellington in the Peninsula and who lived at Brent Lodge, Hanwell. Another distinguished Hanwellian was the artist Frederick Yeames who lived at No. 8 Campbell Road between 1895 and 1912 and who was also churchwarden at St Mary's for a number of years. Yeames' most famous painting is the historical one, *And when did you last see your father?*, which depicts a brave lad being questioned by the Roundheads in order that they may capture his Royalist father. Derwent Coleridge, the son of the poet Samuel Taylor

Coleridge, was Rector of St Mary's, Hanwell, between 1864 and 1880. He made a number of changes, such as the building of St Mark's church, introducing Hymns ancient and modern and starting a choir.

Local newspapers were founded in both parishes. In Southall there was *The Southall News*, which lasted from 1885-1888, by Charles Abbott, which gave its proprietor free rein to attack his enemies. Other local newspapers were *The Southall-Norwood Gazette* and *The Hanwell Gazette*, both founded in 1898. These both carried much news from the longer-established *The Middlesex County Times*, but with a local slant.

Other amenities were being developed as the towns of Hanwell and Southall grew. The shops up to 1839 had been basic; in Southall there were thirty-six shops and tradesmen, mostly bakers, butchers, grocers and boot-makers. By the 1890s, both the number and the variety of shops in both places had risen with the demand. There were over 100 shops and tradesmen in both Hanwell and Southall in 1894. Apart from the basic shops which had risen in number, there were tailors, drapers, hairdressers, banks, watchmakers and even a pianoforte tuner.

Queen Victoria's Diamond Jubilee was celebrated in 1897, marking sixty years on the throne. In Southall, a committee was formed to organize the celebrations. They decided upon a treat for the old people and the children and to erect six almshouses as a permanent reminder of the Queen's reign. In order to raise the necessary funds, a subscription was begun and citizens promised sums of money. Unfortunately, not enough were raised. William Welch Deloitte of Hill House, Mount Pleasant, the founder of a major accountancy firm and already known for his philanthropy, donated more money so that the almshouses could be built and a treat for the elderly given. The almshouses were known as the Deloitte almshouses and are located in North Road, near Mount Pleasant. Deloitte died in 1898 and his widow administered the necessary funds, endowing them with gifts of money and coals.

One Mrs Phillips recalled the celebrations in Hanwell thus:

> The Queen's Diamond Jubilee came along, and was looked forward to by everyone including our cat, who gave birth to three kittens that very morning – so they brought their labels with them; Victoria, Diamond and Jubilee… it was a lovely summers day – and we went up to Walpole Park, and there were stands full of schoolchildren singing *Sixty Years of High Endeavour*. The combined singing of Ealing and/or Hanwell juveniles was very painful.

Like Southall, Hanwell celebrated the Jubilee in a practical way, too. It was decided to found a Cottage Hospital, 'as a philanthropic and practical scheme of general utility, and as a fitting memorial of the Diamond Jubilee

Jubilee celebrations at Hanwell Park, 1887.

of Her Majesty's Reign'. Funds were collected and in 1899 the Countess of Jersey laid the foundation stone. The Hospital was on Green Lane and served both inpatients and outpatients. Treatment was not free, however, and patients from labourers' families had to pay four shillings for inpatients, those from clerks' families, six shillings. In its first year, 1900-1901, thirty-two inpatients were treated, twenty-eight of whom were cured and there had been eleven outpatients. Initially the president and treasurer of this privately-financed charity was Sir Montagu Sharpe.

Queen Victoria's death in January 1901 was marked locally, in a way that previous monarchs were not. Armstrong, residing in Southall, referred to hearing the guns go off at Windsor Castle when George IV died in 1830, but there was no local notice of this event. In 1901, the reaction was different. Local organizations cancelled or cut short meetings to mark the national mourning for the loss of the Queen. At a meeting of Hanwell Council, Mr Walter Abbott, the vice chairman, noted, 'I am sorry to say we have had it announced the poor Queen has gone. I beg to move the adjournment of this council; from further business tonight… out of respect for the occasion'. Mr Williams, the vice-chairman, concurred, 'I think you are acting quite right.'

Hanwell and Southall had made significant strides in the nineteenth century. They were no longer pleasant country villages, but rapidly expanding towns. Agriculture was on the wane, though it had not yet vanished, and industrial concerns were beginning to make themselves felt. Social and spiritual needs were not neglected, as the growing number of sports clubs and churches attest. The municipal life of these towns was also apparent. Urban District Councils, with many new powers, were also having their effect in providing proper lighting, drainage and other amenities.

CHAPTER 6
The Edwardian Age and the First World War, 1901-1918

Although this chapter covers the smallest date span, these years were very important for the development of both Hanwell and Southall. Perhaps most significantly, the population rose in both districts by the largest percentage ever – doubling, in fact, from 1901-1911. A great many new houses were built in response to this and perhaps in anticipation of the demand too. Transport improved, as tramways began to be put into operation. New schools and churches appeared on the scene. The world of entertainment was transformed by the advent of the cinemas and this was the heyday of clubs and societies aimed at the middle and working classes. Southall became a hub of industry. National events which also had a local impact, were two new monarchs, the end of the second Boer War, and, perhaps most important of all, the First World War.

Edward VII, from whose name this period is known, became King and Emperor in January 1901 and the Coronation occurred on 9 August 1902. It was marked in Southall by guns firing, a children's party in Southall Park, and a carnival organized by the town's tradesmen. The town's bands were out in force and the carnival procession marched around Norwood Green and from there to Southall Park, singing *God Save the King*. Shops and houses were decorated with flags and bunting. Although there were some showers, the weather failed to dampen enthusiasm. The day ended with fireworks brightening up the sky.

There was another cause for celebration in 1902. The Second Boer War, which had begun in South Africa in 1899 initially did not go well for Britain, who was trying to fight a regular war against an irregular enemy. With the arrival of fresh armies and the gallant defence of towns such as Ladysmith and Mafeking, the tide began to turn. Mrs Phillips recalled events from the Hanwell perspective.

The Boer War came along – and the newspapers in the [Ealing] Library were a great help towards trying to get at the rights and wrongs of it. I was very sorry for the Boers – but every one was in the swim for buying picture buttons of the British Generals. On Mafeking Night, we joined in a procession making for Ealing Common, singing an abusive song about the Kaiser, all the way, I believe there was a big bonfire, but we had worrying parents to return to. We couldn't get to London, when the City Imperial

Southall Town Hall and fire station, 1907.

Volunteers came home – but bought emblems consisting of natural ivy leaf, with 'C' painted on it in red. Those Generals 'Mine' was Redvers Buller, and of course Baden-Powell – Kitchener, Ian Hamilton and others were on sale – each of whom is still remembered.

Three Southall men who fought in the Boer War received a civic welcome on their return in 1902. Hanwell's fire engine went to London to bring back two local heroes on Peace Night in 1902. One of these men was Hopkins, who had been in the City Imperial Volunteers and the other was a sailor, Alf Peara.

The Urban District Councils continued in their work. They were each made up of twelve elected members, all men, of course, though propertied women could vote in local elections. They had a number of committees, in Hanwell's case, these were, the Fire brigade, Works, Public Lighting, Sanitary, General Purposes, Finance, Library and Farm committees (the two last named committees met infrequently). However, on the Hanwell Library committee in 1911, there were two women, out of a committee total of twelve. Principal council officers were the clerk, treasurer, surveyor and assistant, medical officer, sanitary inspector, rate collector, collector of private street improvements and the librarian.

Both Hanwell and Southall could boast of having a fire service. Hanwell's fire brigade headquarters was located behind the council's offices in Cherington Road. There was a crew of seventeen men and their equipment included a steamer, a hand fire escape, a hose truck and ladders and belts. Southall's fire brigade was initially under the command of Charles Thomas Abbott, from a prominent local family. In 1901 the fire station was built next to the town hall. Hanwell's fire engine was a particular source of local pride and affection. Mr Troy recalled, 'the Fire Engine turned out for almost everything.' They played a prominent part in local celebrations of King George V's Coronation.

The populations of Hanwell and Southall in 1901 were 10,438 and 12,499 respectively, and by 1911 they stood at 19,129 and 26,323 (estimated at 29,343 in 1913). This increase was probably in part because of the attraction of new industries to Southall and also to better transport links to London and elsewhere, allowing more of Southall and Hanwell's residents to commute to work. It was also due to soaring birth rates which far exceeded death rates. For example, between February 1909 and February 1910, 488 babies were born in Hanwell while 165 people died (some from scarlet fever and diptheria).

The London United Tramways Company eventually won the right to run trams through Ealing in 1901 from Ealing Council, who had initially been in opposition to the scheme, wanting to run their own municipal

Trams at Hanwell,
c. 1906.

*Tram at Hanwell on the
Brentford route,
c. 1910.*

tram service. Both Hanwell and Southall councils had approved of such a
measure, though the former council had taken some time to deliberate
over the matter, before coming to a unanimous decision. Trams ran from
Shepherd's Bush through Ealing and Hanwell to Southall from 10 July
1901. Further additions were made in the coming years; Southall to
Uxbridge in 1904 and Brentford to Hanwell along the Boston and Lower
Boston Road by 1906. In 1911, fares from Ealing Broadway to Hanwell were
one penny, and one and a half pennies to Southall Town Hall. Workmen's
fares were at a reduced rate, one penny from Southall to Shepherd's Bush,
for example, but the journey had to be made prior to eight o'clock in the
morning.

The tramways may have helped create a demand for working class and
lower middle class houses in Hanwell. Hanwell Park, which dates back
to the early eighteenth century at least, was demolished in 1913,
completing the process of the breaking up of the estate, and semi-
detached and terraced housing rapidly took its place. All the land
between the Uxbridge Road and the railway was built upon, with the
exception of a small park, Conolly Dell (named after Dr John Conolly,
whose house, The Lawns, had been nearby). North of the railway,
Greenford Avenue was built and other streets and houses were built
nearby. Building was also going on apace along the Boston Road,
spreading further south on both sides. On the western side, the sewage
works prevented any further sprawl southwards.

In Southall, the story was much the same. Much, though not all, of the
land both south and north of the Broadway was built upon, with rows of
houses in both directions. Older houses, such as the eighteenth-century
Townsend House, were demolished. Dr George MacDonald was critical
of some of this housing, and, writing in 1910, referred to 'the jerry
builder' being responsible for the demolition of so many old landmarks.

Conolly Dell, Hanwell, c. 1912.

The settlement around South Road, on both sides of the railway, expanded westwards and eastwards. There was a solid swathe of buildings from the railway to the canal branch to the south. Norwood, though, seemed less affected.

Many other contemporary critics elaborated on MacDonald's views. They tended to deplore the fact that most of the buildings in Southall were modern and poorly built, and that the countryside was being eaten up. This was rather unfortunate from an architectural point of view. These views were echoed in the 1920s and '30s, too.

Some of the open places were, however, being saved. There had as yet been no building from Southall Park to Hanwell Bridge, along the Uxbridge Road. Possibly the asylum acted as a deterrent. The opening of the Brent Valley Golf Course in 1910 saved part of the land to the west of St Mary's, Hanwell. Charles Short, in his book, *Southall and its Environs* (1910) spoke glowingly of this; 'The golf links are on one of the most natural sporting grounds in the country, and occupy more than two hundred acres'. Another park in Hanwell was Elthorne Park, to the south of the Uxbridge Road, which was opened a year later. Conolly Dell was another small open space, just south of the railway line. Southall Council purchased land to form its first public park, the Recreation Ground, which featured a bandstand and a swimming bath in 1902, and another, Southall Park, which was opened in 1909.

The parks were good places to hold public ceremonies and other functions. On the Coronation Day of King George V, 22 June 1911, there was a children's party held in Southall Park. Each child was given a medal to commemorate the event. Similarly, Churchfields Park was used for celebrations in Hanwell, with a speech by the chairman of the Council, musical entertainment and a display by the fire brigade.

There were two cinemas in Hanwell by 1911, The Coronation, at No. 90 Uxbridge Road and the Grand, later the Curzon, on Cherington Road. There was also the Southall Electric Theatre, later known as The Gem, on the corner of Featherstone Road. Tickets cost three pence and one penny for the matinee performances. The Empire and The Palace were two other cinemas which opened in Southall in this period, though the former closed in 1916, apparently because of the risqué nature of the entertainment shown. Hanwell boasted a theatre, too, the Park Theatre, in Greenford Avenue.

The burgeoning number of clubs and societies covered most tastes, sporting, intellectual, political or artistic. In Hanwell, the only party political organization was the Conservative and Unionist Association, and its chairman was the lawyer and historian, Sir Montagu Sharpe (1856-1942), but there was a Southall Working Men's Club, which met in premises on Featherstone Road. There were also several football and cricket clubs. In Hanwell, there were many slate clubs and benefit societies. These were organizations which people paid regular small sums in return for benefits should accidents or mishaps occur to themselves or their families. Most were attached to churches or pubs. Yet, compared to the middle class suburb of Ealing, Hanwell and Southall had less clubs and societies, and of a more limited choice. There were twenty-five political organizations in Ealing and only two in Hanwell in 1911 for example.

This era also saw the beginnings of more secular youth organizations (earlier movements such as the Church Lads were firmly religious in orientation). Chief among these were the Boy Scouts, which had been founded by the hero of Mafeking, General Robert Baden-Powell, in 1907. The First Norwood Scout Troop, Lady Jersey's Own, was founded in 1910. Some were attached to churches, such as the Trinity Church Scouts which Southall resident Richard Meads was a member of – the troop went on its first camp at Long Crendon in July 1914. In August 1916, a thirteen-year-old Hanwell Boy Scout lost his life when trying to rescue two boys from the Brent. His bravery was commemorated by a stained-glass window in St Mellitus' church, Hanwell.

The shops increased in number and variety in Hanwell, though for really fancy goods, a trip to Ealing was necessary. At Southall, too, the shops were adequate for the everyday needs of the populace, but not of the sort which would draw custom from elsewhere. In fact, Richard Meads recalled that Brentford and West Ealing were where Southall folk went to do their main shopping, especially for the Sunday joint. Children were entranced by the Penny Bazaar in West Ealing. At Christmas time, for a special treat, the Meads family would travel up

Sir Montagu Sharpe and deer hound, c. 1901.

Southall Broadway,
c. 1910.

to Shepherd's Bush by tram. Of course, a great deal of shopping was done on the doorstep, as tradesmen came to call. These included not just the milkman, but the grocer, coal man, hardware man and oil man.

For intellectual needs, a Carnegie Library was opened in Hanwell on Cherington Road in 1905 (the same year as the Carnegie Library in Southall was opened, too). Frank Pocock was appointed as the first Librarian. Mrs Phillips recalled the library with fond regard:

> The Hanwell Carnegie Library was a great pleasure – and everything was so simple with cardboard backed catalogues – and one had to pick a book, note its number, and see from the indicator (which enclosed the Librarian), if it was in or out [library books were not then on open access]. I was a great fan of Mrs Henry Wood.

The Lending Library was open from 10 a.m. to 9 p.m. every weekday except Bank Holidays and it closed early on Thursdays. By 1917, there were 5,000 volumes in circulation. A Public Library was built in Southall in 1904. There was also an expansion of church building of the part of all major denominations. St Mellitus' church was built in Hanwell in 1910, the parish having been formed in 1908. Just along the same road (Church Road) was the Methodist church, which had been in the Lower Boston Road, until 1904. St George's church, Southall, was built in 1906. The King's Hall, the centre of Methodism in the district, was built on South Road, Southall, in 1916. The churches were involved in more than just spiritual affairs. For example, in 1911, St Mary's Hanwell, had a number of other organisations under its aegis; the Mothers' Union, Girls' Friendly Society, Church Lads' Brigade, a Men's Institute, to name but a few. St Joseph's church ran a boys' gymnasium on Wednesday evenings, at St

Joseph's school. Clergymen were often active in secular affairs – the Revd S.W. Allen was one of Hanwell's councillors in 1911. In both Hanwell and Southall, clergymen were managers of the local schools.

This was a period of frenetic building, not only of houses and churches, but also of schools. There were four new schools in Hanwell at this time. The first was Catholic, started by the Sisters of St Joseph in 1901. It moved into new buildings on York Avenue in 1908. Middlesex County Council enlarged the old National School, renaming it St Mark's, and built other schools, on Oaklands Road (1906) and on the Greenford Avenue (1911). There was also St Ann's, built in 1902. Similarly, nine new elementary schools were built in Southall between 1901 and 1911.

Apart from this vast growth in elementary schools, a County Grammar School opened in Southall in 1907, with seventy-six pupils, though ten years later, there were 300. It was built on Villiers Road, but served Hanwell and Greenford as well. This was the school for the elite, though

Southall Library, Osterley Park Road, c. 1905.

Procession to Our Lady and St Joseph church, c. 1910.

there were a small number of private schools in Southall at this time, too. The grammar school was for fee payers, and there were only three scholarships at first.

One national event which began in this era and continued for several decades was the celebration of Empire Day, which was on 24 May, Queen Victoria's birthday. Typically, the morning's school lessons were devoted to a celebration of the Empire, songs were sung and in the afternoon, a half holiday was granted. Richard Meads, a Southall resident, who was born in 1904, remembers that this was a day to look forward to. At Clifton Road Boys' School, on this date, the Headmaster, Mr Roger Elias recorded, 'The boys were assembled in the Hall at 3.45, I spoke to them about Empire Day and the National Anthem was played by the band and the boys sang the first verse'.

Although industry in Hanwell was limited, it grew in Southall, marking a divergence between the two districts, following trends which had been evident in the nineteenth century. In 1906 the parish was described as being, 'a manufacturing district'. A little group of large factories sprang into being to the south of the railway. These were an emulsion works, an engineering motor works, a telephone works, a paper mill, a jam factory and the Rubastic Works. A marmalade factory opened on Brent Road in 1913 and the old Norwood Mill was converted into a picture frame moulders. Traditional industries continued, at least for the time being, a new brick-field in North Road opening in 1910, and the East Acton Brick Company was still in business. All these works were at the edges of the district, not close to the housing, which was ever-expanding. Hanwell had some small industries, such as the British Ebonite Company and an engineering firm in Church Road.

The Otto Monsted Works, evermore attentive to the needs of its workers, built the Maypole Institute, at the cost of £14,000, for their benefit. This centre provided a staff canteen and rooms for rest, relaxation and indoor games. However, at work, discipline was firm, with a ban on smoking or drinking alcohol at work. Working hours were long; six in the morning to six at night and no tea breaks. During this period, the factory expanded considerably; two artesian wells were sunk, there were sidings leading to the dairy, office extensions, as well as the dock to the canal as mentioned in chapter four.

Agriculture seems to have declined even further. However, the number of allotments seems to have risen. By 1914, there were six of them throughout Southall and two in Hanwell. There were also several local dairies which supplied local houses with milk and other dairy products. One such was Mr J.T. Edwards, at No. 114 Uxbridge Road, and another was Walter John Blackwell, who had three premises in Hanwell. Glebe and Waxlow farms still operated in Southall. There were also suppliers of agricultural goods in Southall for the Cattle Market.

Milking of cows near St Mary's church, Hanwell, c. 1900s.

The Edwardian Age came to an end in 1910 with the death on 9 May of the King. The local newspapers used heavy black ink to indicate their sorrow. As well as generous editorials in the press, two local people, Mr Henly of Southall and Emily Langley of Hanwell, wrote poems in tribute to the late monarch. Edward VII was known as the Peacemaker, and in one verse of her poem, Emily Langley commented on this:

> Thy life has been a bright and kingly one,
> For thee perchance regret may never cease
> A brave good gentleman who wielded well,
> What England needed most – the wand of peace.

At Clifton Road School, Mr Elias wrote thus in the log:

The staff and boys have heard with great regret of the sad death of His Majesty the King and the flag in the yard was hoisted to half mast. Instructions have been given to the teachers to give the appropriate lessons on the sad calamity, his life and that of his son who succeeds him.

Four years later, peace was no more; ninety-nine years of general peace in Europe were broken. Britain declared war on Germany on 4 August 1914, following Germany's aggression against Britain's Entente allies, France and Russia. A recruiting party marched through Ealing and Hanwell, picking up men for the Eighth Battalion of the Middlesex Regiment. Reservists and Territorials were quickly called up. The

Church encouraged men to join. At St Mellitus' in August there was a recruiting drive; *Land of Hope and Glory* being played on the organ. Sergeant Lewis of No. 80 Uxbridge Road, was the chief recruiter for Hanwell and Southall. Often men who worked together joined together – there were fifty-sixty men from the Gasworks in Southall, four men from the Hanwell post sorting office, and 463 men from the Otto Monsted Factory (fifty-two men from the latter were killed).

That the war would be devastating was acknowledged in the press at the onset, as the editorial in *The Hanwell Gazette* observed, on 8 August 1914. It would be 'An Armageddon, the terrible possibilities of which overshadow all the desolation and misery wrought by the Napoleonic Wars [1793-1815]'. Park school, Hanwell, was used as a hospital for Belgian soldiers. Two buildings in Southall were used as military hospitals: the Maypole Institute (offered to the government by the company in 1915) and St Marylebone school. The latter was used as a hospital for Australian soldiers, which led to two developments. Firstly, many of the soldiers who recovered married local girls and they returned to Australia after the war. Secondly, the Australian government presented the Southall British Legion with two captured German field guns afterwards, in recognition of the town's services to its young men. Unsurprising, given the hostility towards all names German, The King of Prussia pub changed its name to The Victory.

A Southall man who became a local war hero was Captain (later General) Frank Crowther Roberts, son of the vicar of St John's. He was a professional soldier, having been commissioned in 1911. He won a DSO in 1915 and the Military Cross in 1917. In March 1918, at the time when the German army was making its last desperate push for victory before the

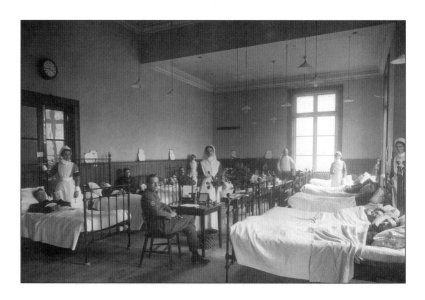

Ward in Otto Monsted Hospital, 1916.

Nurses in the pharmacy of Otto Monsted Hospital, c. 1916.

American forces could make an impact, Roberts was with his battalion (The Worcester Regiment) at Pargny, west of the Somme. At the time he was acting Lieutenant Colonel. During the orderly retreat, Roberts led a counter-attack against the enemy, which helped cover the retreat. For his 'conspicuous bravery' and 'exceptional military skill' he won the Victoria Cross. Fortunately Roberts survived the war.

Around 3,500 Southall men joined the various branches of His Majesty's Forces, mostly the Army, and in particular, the Middlesex battalions. This was a large proportion, amounting to about 25% of the total male population. Eight hundred men were killed. If this seems a high casualty figure, which it certainly was, one should consider that casualty rates were even higher in France, Russia and Germany, though this was no consolation to war widows and mothers.

More prosaically, women took over men's jobs at the Otto Monsted factory in Southall. It is well known that many women began to work in factories and in hospitals during the war, thus helping the cause of women's suffrage far more so than the terrorist activities of the radical fringe of pre-war suffragettes (women over thirty were granted the vote in Parliamentary elections in 1918). What is perhaps less well known is that women were also involved in other roles during the war. Of the thirteen public elementary schools in Southall in 1917, nine were run by school mistresses. The superintendents of the two Poor Law schools in Hanwell were also women.

Elsewhere on the Home Front, the danger of air raids became a worry as Zeppelins bombed London in 1915-1916. However, the local authorities decided not to build any shelters, stating that the danger was minimal; in the event of a raid, people should merely stay indoors or seek shelter if outside. Such views were justified by events. Some

Victory celebrations at Southall gasworks, 1919.

public buildings were reinforced by sandbagging and were designated as shelters, though. Apart from this, the only hardship for the civilian population was the introduction of rationing, which did not occur until 1917, though food had been becoming scarce in 1916; in Germany and Russia, food shortages were worse.

Peace was initially welcomed by low-key celebrations. At Tudor Road school, on 11 November 1918, the Headmaster noted, 'Today the Armistice was signed and after celebrations in the school a half holiday was given'. In Hanwell, there was a civic celebration of peace at St Mellitus', in November 1918. There was a procession of civic dignitaries, the fire brigade (of course!), the Special Constabulary, and the Salvation Army Band, flanked by Scouts and Guides. The church was packed, and singing began with *Onward Christian Soldiers* before prayers of thanksgiving were intoned by the Revd Leonard Spillar. One man who was arrested in Hanwell for being drunk and disorderly on Armistice Night was let off with a caution, given what day it was. Official celebrations occurred in 1919.

The fallen were commemorated in public by a solid, Cenotaph-like memorial outside Southall Manor House which was unveiled in 1922, as well as other, smaller and more specific memorials in schools and churches. Otto Monsted's factory compiled a book in memory of the dead, with pictures of each, lest future generations forget their sacrifice. Hanwell did not, unlike neighbouring Southall, Greenford or Ealing, have a town war memorial. However, there was a memorial in the Cottage hospital in 1923, which henceforth became known as 'The Queen Victoria and War Memorial Hospital'. The local Scouts, who had helped guard reservoirs and other useful wartime duties, put a memorial up to their brother Scouts who had fallen in the struggle, in Churchfields Recreation Park, as well as planting an avenue of chestnut trees in the same park. Churches also contained war memorials.

The pre-war period is often seen in retrospect, as a halcyon golden age, given the carnage of the war and the unsettled peace which followed it. This is very much with the benefit of hindsight. As we have seen, the pre-war years were anything but calm. They were a period of frenetic change and activity in many fields; transport, housing, education, industry and building, which may have proved unsettling to some. Many contemporary critics certainly disapproved of the changes which were taking place. Change had certainly happened at a faster rate either before or since, but it had been necessary and for the most part beneficial.

Southall war memorial.

CHAPTER 7
The Inter War Years and the Second World War, 1918-1945

There were a number of significant developments in Hanwell and Southall during this period. Administratively, Hanwell was absorbed by Ealing whilst Southall's municipal progress was recognised in its gaining borough status. In both districts housing, population and public services increased. Industry in Southall grew, too. Trams were replaced by trolley buses and motor buses made their first appearance on local roads. There was strife, too, with the challenge from the Left with the General Strike and later from the Right, in the form of Fascism. Overshadowing both of these dangers was the Second World War.

Almost as soon as the First World War was over, Lloyd George's Coalition government called a General Election, the first in eight years. Neither Hanwell nor Southall were Parliamentary constituencies in their own right. Southall was now part of the Uxbridge constituency and Hanwell part of Harrow. At an election address of the Conservative and Unionist Party at Oaklands Road school in November 1918, presided over by Sir Montagu Sharpe, the Party's youthful candidate aired his policies. That candidate was a former soldier, Lieutenant Oswald Mosley (1896-1980). He spoke of the need for the state to intervene in the economy to help returning soldiers and to improve their lives and to better the lot of women, too. He was elected. However, his future career was somewhat chequered. In 1922 he became a Labour MP and in 1931 he formed the British Union of Fascists (BUF).

In 1923, *The Hanwell Gazette* ceased to publish. Worse was to follow. Hanwell lost its municipal status in 1926. Along with Greenford, it was incorporated into its large neighbour, Ealing. This was being discussed in 1923 by Ealing Council, who had written to the government about the possibility of increasing its borough boundaries. The government thought that there were too many small authorities in London and so agreed with Ealing Council in principle. It was believed that such a move would benefit Ealing, both socially and municipally, and that it would help local businesses. Ealing's mayor, Councillor David Howell-Jones, thought that the people of Hanwell had already concluded that 'A separate existence for them as a local government unit was no longer desirable'. Certainly, in the council elections, all Hanwell candidates had

*West Middlesex Golf
Links, 1920s.*

pledged themselves to amalgamation with Ealing. It was decided to hold
a meeting of all interested parties.

Although there was still discussion by Hanwell Council over these
proposals in 1925, by the following year, the decision had been made. On
26 September 1926, there was the last civic procession of the councillors,
the band, the fire brigade and others. They marched around Hanwell and
arrived at St Mary's church, which was packed to capacity. The vicar, the
Revd William Farquhar, made some interesting observations. He said
that, 'in future the ancient name of Hanwell would be merely a
geographical expression.' He added that, 'the enlarged borough held
magnificent possibilities for the welfare of its inhabitants, but they could
not help feeling a twinge of regret at the passing out of existence of
Hanwell as a separate entity.'

There were some links between Hanwell and Ealing already; Hanwell
residents used some of Ealing council's services, such as the swimming
baths and the Isolation Hospital. Hanwell, being a small district, could
not afford such amenities. However, that did not eliminate the bitterness
which some local people felt at being 'taken over' by Ealing. Mr Troy, in
his reminiscences, written in 1944, wrote, 'It was a knock-out blow to our
old Hanwellites when Ealing Borough literally pinched the Fire Engine
from us in 1926 and also the Trophies which we managed to get back.
Hanwell has never been the same to us since.' Ealing Council was
petitioned for the return of the fire engine to Hanwell, but to no avail.
Certainly, Ealing's mayor had believed that a unified Fire Service at
Ealing would be a useful economy to make, and this had been public
knowledge since 1923. Yet if Hanwellians had anyone to blame, it was
their councillors.

Hanwell fire engine, 1920s.

After amalgamation, Hanwell was politically represented at council level by six councillors, three in each ward (south and north), out of a full council of thirty-six councillors. In 1937, two of the twelve aldermen were from Hanwell, one being the deputy mayor, too, John Lynch. The other alderman was a woman, Mrs Emily Sophia Taylor, JP. She had been the first woman chairman of the old Hanwell Council, in 1919. She had been a teacher and was fond of motoring and church work among children.

In 1936, Southall gained its borough charter and became an incorporated borough. This meant that it gained in municipal status, having a coat of arms and a mayor, instead of a mere chairman. William Garrod was the Charter Mayor and Charles Pryce Abbott, his deputy. In order to gain borough status, the council had to compile a dossier of information about Southall, detailing its population, its industries, municipal services, social amenities and other facts. The Charter was granted and signed by the new King, Edward VIII.

Charter Day, 24 September, was accompanied by a great many festivities in Southall Park. However, it was not without controversy. The new name for the borough was Southall, whereas the old name of the Urban District Council was Southall-Norwood, and the exclusion of Norwood offended some. After all, Norwood was the name of the old parish in which Southall had been a mere hamlet. As opposed to that, from the nineteenth century at least, the main centre of population and industry had been Southall, whereas Norwood had remained as a rural hamlet and so could be hardly said to reflect the modern district.

Politically, the new borough of Southall was mostly, though not overwhelmingly, Labour. Although the Parliamentary constituency to which it belonged returned Conservative or National (coalition, but predominantly Conservative) Government candidates, the council had a Labour majority. Its local opposition came, not from the Conservatives or the declining number of Liberals, but from the Independent Rate Payers' Party, which, if not exactly Conservative, was 'definitely anti-Socialist' and tried to curb increases in council spending and thus keep the rates at a reasonable level. Their rancour at the Labour majority led to their chairman, Charles Pryce Abbott, to declare that, in the 1930s, there was a dictatorship in local affairs worse than that in Germany (when Hitler was in power).

Trophies won by Hanwell fire brigade, 1928.

Despite such political opposition, the council was doing what most thought to be useful work. A branch library, Jubilee Gardens, was opened in 1938, opposite a new health clinic and park. These were necessary due to the increasing building that was occurring to the north of the borough. Another recreation ground was opened in the north-west of the borough, the Municipal Recreation Ground at Spike's Bridge, which was designed for the playing of team games. This was opened by Lord Farringdon, a Labour peer, in 1937. Another health clinic was based at the Chestnuts, Southall Green from 1935 and there were council offices in the old Manor House.

Secondary schools and a Technical college were established in Southall at this time. Schools opened at Dormers Wells, Featherstone Road and the Western Road. The Technical college opened on Beaconsfield Road in 1928. This was for boys in the daytime and there were evening classes for young men. It taught engineering technology in the classroom and laboratories. Extensions were built in the 1930s.

Both councils, Hanwell and Southall, were busy trying in their own small ways to make 'Homes Fit for Heroes'. Most of the houses which had been built before the war, and afterwards, too, had been by speculative

William Garrod and Mrs Garrod, Charter Mayor and Mayoress of Southall, 1936.

Southall's mace, 1936.

private builders. The Housing Act of 1919 allowed Hanwell Council to build 122 houses and flats in Townholme Crescent and an estate of thirty houses in Montague Road and Cambridge Road. These last, though, were completed under the aegis of Ealing council after 1926. By 1939, Southall council had built 1,119 homes. Southall's population continued to grow, though at a slower rate than it had just prior to the First World War; from 30,287 in 1921 to an estimated 52,680 in 1939.

The building of new housing continued afresh. The Central London District School, which was now run by the London County Council, was knocked down in 1933, apart from the central block which was to be used as a community centre. By 1939, 1,592 council houses had been built on its grounds. However, although housing expanded, on both sides of the Uxbridge Road, the boundaries to the west of the Brent and to the east with the two cemeteries, helped reinforce a sense of local community. Two new Anglican churches were built, St Thomas' in 1934 and St Christopher's in 1937. New council schools were also built to cater for the increasing number of children.

In Southall, the story was the same. Over 700 houses were built to the north of the district in the 1920s, chiefly in Mount Pleasant and near Allenby Road, towards Greenford to the north and towards Hanwell to the east. Building also occurred to the south of the Uxbridge Road, pushing westwards as far as the canal and eastwards between Southall Park and the railway, along the Uxbridge Road. All the land to the south of the railway was built upon, as the boundaries of Southall's building moved westwards, as far as the canal. There was even building in Norwood, with an estate being built between the canal and the houses bordering Norwood Green. Between 1930-1935, 4,000 houses were

Newly-built Ranelagh Road, c. 1930.

constructed. Very little space remained by 1939, and overcrowding was feared in 1944. Most houses were of good quality, too. In 1935, only thirty were condemned as slum dwellings. Many of these houses were relatively inexpensive. Some were within the reach of working families; in 1922, Richard Meads recalls purchasing a house for £345, and this was not an uncommon price in this era. Others lived in rented accommodation.

Two large building firms which did a lot of this work were Taylor Woodrow and George Wimpey & Co., Ltd. The latter had a reputation for sharp practices towards their workforce, allegedly sacking men at an hour's notice in order to encourage the others. According to Richard Meads, when one worker remarked that Rome wasn't built in a day, the foreman replied that it would have been if Wimpey's had had the contract.

Southall had been termed 'a manufacturing district' before the First World War. It became even more of one during the 1920s and 1930s. The reasons for this probably lie in the good transport network of railways and canals, as mentioned in chapter four. But they were also because land and labour were available. Because Southall had been relatively rural in the nineteenth century, there was still space available for the building of factories, despite its spectacular growth in the early twentieth century. Labour was plentiful, given the growing population.

Many firms which were, or became, household names, were located in Southall. These included Crown Cork Company in 1922, AEC (Associated Equipment Company) in 1927, which employed 2,000 people, Taylor Woodrow in 1930 and Quaker Oats in 1936. AEC made London's buses, lorries and other vehicles. It was situated off Windmill Lane, near to the asylum (which was renamed St Bernard's in 1937). Quaker Oats, which produced breakfast cereals and animal fodder, was located in Otto Monsted's old site. Another large firm was G.C. Cross and Co., a building and haulage firm, which moved to Southall in 1919. They prospered from work on the Empire Exhibition at Wembley in 1924. On Lancaster Road was Wimpey's repair and maintenance depot, which employed 400 people.

John Hull Grundy, a young naturalist, was critical of developments taking place under his very nose. In 1924, he observed:

Then again the road is being continued right up "Old" Windmill Lane to Greenford much to the detriment of the beauty of the countryside… Houses now inhabited have been built… thus filling up completely the once stretch of green pasture with its hawthorn and blackberry hedge, and ditch with its glorious tangle of stichwork and teagle, violets and primroses which will soon be gone from the memory of man.

George Orwell has his character George Bowling in *Coming up for Air*, make similar remarks: 'I struck into outer London and followed the Uxbridge Road as far as Southall. Miles and miles of ugly houses, with people living dull, decent lives inside them.'

Briggs, in his book *Middlesex Old and New*, was unsympathetic to this line of reasoning, stating that:

> Regret for this change is quite futile; it has come to stay, and we must accept it. Its effects are not so disastrous as in some of the northern strongholds of nineteenth century industrialism, because electric power has largely eliminated smoke, and most modern factories, designed to produce a large output from contented workers, are a great advance on those which made England prosperous fifty years ago.

It is difficult not to sympathise with Grundy and Orwell, while agreeing with Briggs.

It was not only physical change which occurred. Many other institutions, which served as reminders of the past, but which had little or no practical role, disappeared. Norwood vestry, which had been losing its powers throughout the nineteenth century, was wound up in 1932. Manorial tenure came to an end in 1930 and Lord Hillingdon was the last lord of the manor of Southall. For better or worse, links with the past were being cut away.

Despite the industrial growth, 987 people of Southall were unemployed in 1935, mostly unskilled men and those in the building trade. This was, of course, the time of the depression of the 1930s. Southall's difficulties were exacerbated by some of the unemployed from the west of England and Wales moving to the district in search of work. As Briggs, in *Middlesex: Old and New* wrote, in 1934, Southall's pavements were, 'thronged with immigrants from all parts of Britain, some of whom were Welsh'. Even so, unemployment was far worse in parts of the north of England.

Unlike the residents of Southall, most of those in Hanwell did not work in local factories. In 1921, 136 were employed in gardening and agriculture. However, of the 8,800 working population, almost 5,800, worked outside the district. As the local press remarked at the onset of the General Strike (1926), about Hanwell's workforce, 'that large section of the community which has daily to travel to the city to work.' These included some of the 973 who worked in the commercial sector. The second biggest employer of local labour was the transport industry and 927 worked on trains, buses, trams and in associated industries. A total of 448 local women worked as servants, the biggest single employer of

*High Street Southall,
c. 1939.*

women. Yet many women did not go out to work. In 1921, 5,731 (half the total) of women of working age, were not in paid employment. Many would have been looking after children and the home. Local industry was still small-scale. There were a number of small workshops south of the Uxbridge Road which started up in this period. An Iron Works appeared to the east of the canal, near to the sewage works. Although the Hill family left Hanwell in the 1930s, their violin factory remained.

More cinemas were built in Southall; the Dominion and the Odeon in the 1930s. The Palace Cinema was rebuilt, as was the Gem, both in the 1920s. The cinemas, though, did not open on Sundays, when many young people were otherwise unoccupied, and a debate about Sunday opening arose. It was argued that these places should be opened to give the young people something to do and to prevent them from becoming a public nuisance. Others thought that bad behaviour should not go rewarded.

Trolleybuses were first seen on the roads in 1931 and by 1936 had replaced trams in Southall and Hanwell – though they, nevertheless, continued to serve much of London until 1952. Motor buses first came to Southall in 1923. The first route went as far as Hither Green in South London, and the cost of the full journey was one shilling and seven pence. In 1935, there were five bus routes through Southall and one Sunday service. Many of the first buses were one man enterprises, but these were taken over by the end of the twenties by the London and General Omnibus Company, itself incorporated into London Transport in 1933. Motor cars became a more familiar sight and were now no longer the preserve of the rich, but were being driven by professional people such as teachers. However, according to John Hull Grundy, travelling by road could be a hazardous business, as he observed on 4 July 1923, 'The Uxbridge Road from Southall to Hanwell Broadway had been a positive disgrace and danger to anyone riding a bicycle and even very uncomfortable for the occupants of motor or motorcycle'. This was because the roads were in a poor state.

Hanwell Broadway, during the 1920s.

Little did most people know it, but a future celebrity was born in Southall in 1927. This was Cleo Laine, the jazz singer. Her father had served with the West Indian Expeditionary Force in the First World War and later married an English girl. They settled in Southall. Cleo went to Featherstone Road infants' school and she and her sister also had private dancing lessons. The only other known black woman residing locally was Grace Stevenson, 'a native of Jamacia' who had been appointed by Hanwell council as head nurse in 1918.

The General Strike took place from 4-14 May 1926. Although its origins lay in an industrial dispute between miners and coal owners, it assumed a more universal character. Many saw it as a struggle between the democratic government of Britain and the forces of organized labour led by the Trades Union Congress; alarmists talked about revolution. The actual effect on the ground was that drivers of trams, buses and trains refused to work. The country was in danger of grinding to a halt.

The government took steps to counter this, and one way in which it did so was to call for volunteers. In order to register and organize them, Ealing Town Hall was designated as the centre of a number of districts, including Hanwell and Southall. These volunteers were not strike breakers, though some thought otherwise, but helped to maintain essential transport and supply services. In Southall, an Emergency Committee was formed to ensure adequate supplies of coal to households. Skeleton train services were provided and cheers were heard when trains marked 'Food Supplies' arrived. Although the quantity of food was reduced, there was no danger of a serious shortage. However, a few factories in Southall were affected.

Although there were large numbers of men on strike in both Hanwell and Southall, chiefly tram workers and railwaymen, who were on picket duty or in groups on the street, everything was orderly and quiet. The strikers held evening meetings on Hanwell Broadway addressed by Labour politicians. The many people who commuted into work in London were not prevented from doing so, due to volunteers or independent operators manning the trams.

The Strike was called off on 14 May. There had only been two local cases of violence, both minor. Firstly, when Michael Healey, a Southall man, assaulted a policeman. Healey had been noisy and was told to be quiet. When he answered with abuse, he was arrested and he then struck Constable Dowd. Healey was sentenced to three months hard labour. Secondly, some omnibus windows were broken in Hanwell. Generally, though, people had been calm and good humoured. Relief greeted the end of the strike. The Hanwell tram men marched back to the depot, heads held high, singing *The Red Flag*. One Hanwell man lamented the end of the strike – he had been able to get to work in the City at a considerably reduced fare than before the strike began.

The challenge posed by Fascism was also relatively weak and easily stopped in its tracks. There had been an application by the British Union of Fascists in July 1938 to hold public meetings in Southall Park. Although the Labour Council had permitted another extremist group, the Communists, to hold meetings there, they disallowed the use of the park by the Fascists. The Independent Rate Payers minority party on the council opposed this in the interests of free speech. The council's Labour members stated that they were opposed to Fascism and would not allow it anywhere on council property to speak. As they were in the majority, they had their way. Local trades unionists supported this decision. Possibly public order was thought to be in danger, though none had arisen from Sir Oswald Mosley's speech in Ealing earlier that year.

Happily, in an age where political extremism on both the Left and the Right was the sad fate of many of the nations of Europe, the majority of the British people remained essentially moderate. Nowhere was this more obvious than during the celebrations surrounding the Silver Jubilee of King George V, in May 1935. In Hanwell, schools were closed for a week. The children of Oaklands Road Infants school attended a party on 7 May to celebrate the event and were given medals from the county and spoons from the Borough of Ealing to mark the event. The girls at St Ann's secondary school took part in a pageant of country dancing and singing in Walpole Park, Ealing on 6 May. They were also given spoons and medals. There were also scenes of celebration in Southall Park, attended by a record 8,000 people. There was a baby show, sports, band performances, pageant scenes and a bonfire. Senior schoolchildren attended cinema performances, some of which were in colour, which showed Jubilee scenes elsewhere. Even animals displayed their masters' loyalties; a bulldog was seen in the park wearing a Union flag on his back.

The Second World War (1939-1945) was to have a far greater impact on the civilian population than had the First World War. This was because of

Children's celebrations of the Silver Jubilee in Walpole Park, 1935.

the widespread bombing of the civilian population, evacuation of children, the immediate conscription of men into the fighting forces, the introduction of rationing in 1939, and the use of factories to produce weapons. The threat of invasion in summer 1940 led to the removal of place-name signs.

Despite the fact that Southall's industries were largely converted to war use (AEC made parts for thousands of armoured vehicles, tanks and aircraft), they were untouched by enemy bombing. Perhaps because Southall is about nine miles from London it escaped the worst of the bombing. That twenty-two people in the borough were killed was a relatively small price to pay, though 111 were seriously injured and 122 slightly wounded. The neighbouring borough of Ealing lost 304 lives. Often people were indifferent to the danger, as Henry St John wrote in his diary on 2 September 1940, just as the Blitz was beginning: '7.58 a.m. I left Shackleton Road [Southall] and proceeded via Hanwell Broadway (8.10 a.m.) to Hanway House (9a.m.). It was a fine warm day. We were passing Viaduct Field when the conductor indicated that there was a raid, and the sirens shrieked as we ascended the incline to Hanwell Broadway. A man continued to clean the window of a shop in Ealing'.

Bomb damage to housing was more significant, though hardly on a large scale compared to elsewhere. In Southall, thirty-three properties were destroyed, 294 were seriously damaged and 3,124 received lesser harm.

After the Blitz of September 1940 to April 1941, the skies over England were generally quieter until the summer of 1944 with the attacks of the V1 Doodlebugs and V2 rockets. On 19 June, three V1s fell on Southall, killing two people and damaging much property, especially around Tentelow Lane. Four days later, there was extensive damage in Deans Road, Hanwell, though no-one was killed. There were other raids in these districts in July and August, but none thereafter. The attack on 30 August which effected

Regina Road and Adelaide Road was Southall's worst, and, thankfully, last, such experience. No V2 rockets fell on either district.

The evacuation of children was far from universal. Some Hanwell children were sent to Henley on Thames in 1939, but many stayed. The girls of St Ann's secondary school were merely transferred, for a time, to the Cuckoo school in northern Hanwell. Air-raid shelters were constructed in Hanwell schools in early 1940 and were ready by May. When the air raid sirens sounded, which they frequently did in the autumn of that year, the staff and pupils went to the shelters. Children also helped in salvage and savings drives, which were organized by schools as well as by the council.

Alderman Smith greets C. Smith, chair of Southall Savings Committee, 1941.

Salvage drive, 1941.

Southall Salvation Army Band plays in the street on VE Day, 1945.

Southall's motor-driven pump unit, 1940s.

Life on the Home Front was certainly active, too. Salvage Drives, War Weapons' Week and Salute the Soldier Weeks were all designed to raise funds for the war effort. The Borough of Southall raised £477,174 to adopt the destroyer HMS *Boreas*, in 1942, though two years later, she was given to the Greek navy and HMS *Duckworth* was adopted instead.

Four British restaurants were opened in Southall to help feed war workers and other members of the public. Some of them sold takeaway meals, which was then a novel idea. The food was basic but wholesome and helped supplement rations. The Council established a municipal piggery on the site of the old sewage plant near the Brent and encouraged people to grow food on their allotments to help ease the food situation. At the Drill Hall in Featherstone Road, food parcels for allied prisoners of war were packaged to be sent via the Red Cross to prison camps – almost one million were sent from Southall. Interestingly, in light of Southall's post-war history, the centre also helped India House to pack parcels containing atta, flour, curry and dhal for Indian prisoners of war – half a million being sent from here. Six Indian servicemen on their way home to India thanked the helpers personally (as in the First World War, so in the Second, the Indian contribution to the British Empire's war effort was considerable).

When the defeat of Germany was acknowledged on 8 May 1945 (Victory in Europe Day), there were a number of street parties, bonfires, burning Hitler in effigy and so on. The official celebration had to wait until 20 May, and was held in Southall Park. There was more rejoicing in August when the defeat of Japan meant that the World War was over. Apart from such public celebrations, there were more sombre scenes of thanksgiving in the churches.

During the years covered in this chapter, Hanwell and Southall's paths had diverged, but in some ways had remained broadly similar. Hanwell lost its civic status while Southall's municipal prestige had risen. Southall had gained a great deal of heavy industry which provided much local employment. Although a few small scale industries had arisen in Hanwell, most of its working population were employed outside the district. Both districts had expanded, though at a lesser rate than before 1914. Even so, those spaces of open land which made their boundaries with other districts obvious, no longer existed. Little new building could now take place, but this did not mean that stagnation lay ahead. The challenge of the Second World War did not seem to daunt the residents of Southall and Hanwell, and fortunately loss of life and destruction of property were limited.

CHAPTER 8
The Post War World, 1945-2001

In some ways this chapter is the most difficult to write because it covers (at time of writing) the immediate past, for which much information is as yet unavailable. The aim of this chapter is not to be comprehensive – so many important developments have occurred, and, just as crucially, so much information has been produced about them, that to write in detail about any of them, never mind them all, is impossible. The purpose of this chapter is, instead, to present in concise form, a survey of what seem to have been the most important trends of the post-1945 period in Southall and Hanwell. These include post-war rebuilding, the key changes in local government, immigration and the question of suburban decline and possible revival.

Southall became a Parliamentary constituency in 1945 and has ever since returned a Labour member, with varyingly sized majorities. Most have had very long terms of office, though none have as yet achieved ministerial rank. George Pargiter, MP from 1950-1966, was a former Southall mayor. Sidney Bidwell was next, until 1992 The first Indian MP was Piara Khabra, a former general secretary of the Indian Workers' Association who has been MP from 1992 to the date of writing. Despite some local opposition, manifested by the appearance of independent

Sidney Bidwell, Southall MP, with one of his paintings, 1980.

Greenford Road housing estate, Southall, 1949.

candidates in the 2001 election, his majority was only marginally reduced. Southall was a marginal Labour seat in the 1950s and '60s. Since then, it has become one of the safest Labour seats in the country. Hanwell has never been an independent Parliamentary constituency, being part of Harrow to 1945, then briefly part of Ealing East until 1948 when it became part of Southall.

For some years there had been talk of further reform of local government in and around London. This resulted in the Government of London Act of 1963 which created a Greater London Council, abolished the old Middlesex County Council and, most importantly for the subject of this book, made fewer and larger local government authorities. Hanwell had, in 1926, been absorbed into a larger neighbouring borough. There had been a possibility of Southall merging with Hayes, and, indeed, from the historical view this had much to commend itself, as Southall had been part of the manor and later parish of Hayes until 1859.

This was not to be. Southall and Acton were merged with Ealing to form the London Borough of Ealing, which took effect from April 1965. For Southall, twenty-nine years of borough status and 106 of independence were over.

The effect of the amalgamation of 1965 was to shift the administrative centre of Southall to Ealing. It resulted in a degree of centralization of council services – for example, council offices in the Manor House and town hall were vacated. Many have seen this as a distinct disadvantage, and that Southall has been subsequently neglected by a distant Ealing Council. Such charges of neglect were not unique to Southall. Other parts of the borough (and parts of other amalgamated boroughs throughout London) thought likewise. However, these critics should remember that both Hanwell and Southall do send representatives to Ealing Council, and if the latter are at fault, the critics, if local electors, do have the opportunity every four years to vote them out. In 1965, of sixty-six councillors, twelve represented Southall and three represented Hanwell. By the late 1970s, this had changed to fifteen and six respectively. Even so, this number did represent a minority who could be voted down by the more numerous Ealing members.

Post-war Britain was, perhaps, little different from much of the rest of Europe. It had been damaged by six years of war. It looked decidedly unkempt; much work needed to be done in rebuilding the country. Many men had been killed or injured, so there was less available labour to do the necessary work. Southall and Hanwell were no exception. In particular, factories in Southall, like those in other expanding industrial towns, faced a labour shortage.

The 1950s and '60s were generally good economic years for Britain, which was participating in a more general European post-war boom. Hanwell's small scale industries included factories making plastics, laminated glass, sheet metal works, processed flour and water purifying apparatus. On a lighter note, locations were used in Hanwell for two of the popular *Carry On* British comedy films; *Carry on Constable* (1960) and *Carry on Teacher* (1962). The pop group, Deep Purple, recorded some of their music in Hanwell Community Centre in 1969.

Large-scale industry in Southall was also booming in these years, with some firms expanding and taking on more workers. For example, AEC grew, employing 5,000 workers in 1961, making it Southall's biggest single employer. Taylor Woodrow also expanded in Southall in the 1950s. In 1956, slightly over half of the working population were employed in vehicle or food production, or in supplying water, gas or electricity.

Although Southall had escaped the worst of the bombing, one of the most pressing problems facing the council (as with every local authority in Britain) was the housing shortage, caused both by bombing and by general neglect due to six years of total war.

Some people were resettled in Bracknell or the other new towns built around London in the 1950s. For those who did not leave, the council built more houses, including low rise flats, some of which were opened on the north of the Uxbridge Road, towards Dormers Wells Lane in 1953. Between 1945 and 1958, 530 houses, 438 flats and thirty-five old peoples' dwellings were constructed.

Out of the blue, almost literally, a transport disaster struck Southall on the morning of 2 September 1958. A Viking airliner of Independent Travel Ltd, coming from London Airport, crashed onto houses in Kelvin Gardens. Seven were killed (including three children) and eight injured. Given that the aircraft crashed on residential property, it was a miracle that the casualty figure was so low. Fire and civil defence personnel

Blocks of flats, Golf Links estate, late 1960s.

searched the rubble for survivors. It would seem that the aircraft's engines were faulty, though some thought that air traffic control was to blame.

Perhaps if one had to single out the one most important aspect of Southall's (and to a far lesser extent, Hanwell's) post-war history, it would have to be large-scale immigration from the Commonwealth. Of course, as many contemporary writers are quick to point out, this is no new phenomenon. What is different about post-war immigration in Southall was its scale, the subsequent displacement of the indigenous population, the fact that the cultures and religions of the immigrants and their new host nation were very different, and the fact that there had been virtually no non-European immigration into Southall prior to 1945, which had not always been the case in coastal and dockland regions.

Initially Southall attracted immigrants primarily from the Indian sub-continent and the West Indies. At first, their numbers were not particularly noticeable. The 1951 census stated, that, out of a total population of 55,896, only 330 had been born in the Commonwealth, colonies and protectorates (less than 1%). Almost every other Middlesex borough contained more immigrants than Southall. By 1957, numbers had increased as many began to be employed in local factories such as AEC and at Woolf's rubber factory. A story has arisen that it was Woolf's Rubber Factory which was responsible for the large-scale settlement of Indians in Southall. Apparently, a manager of the company had fought alongside Indians during the Second World War and when the factory was in need of labour, asked his contacts in India if they wished to work here. Many did so. This story has been in print since at least 1963, but its authenticity is difficult to verify. The grandson of a former director of the firm told the author that it was a doubtful tale and was racist in origin, having been originally put about in order to blame someone (i.e. Woolf's directors) for Indian immigration into the district.

According to the 1961 census, there were 1,678 residents born in India, 102 from Pakistan and 481 from the West Indies. Most were men. This was out of a falling total population of 52,983. However, in the light of the Notting Hill riots, and the perception that other social and economic problems might be exacerbated by unrestricted immigration, the Immigration Act of 1962 sought to restrict the entry of immigrants into the country; only those with special skills were to be accepted. This led to a rush of immigrants to beat the deadline; by 1965, the number of immigrants in Southall was estimated at between 6,000-9,000, or about 11% of the population, a significant increase.

Numbers rapidly increased as new arrivals headed towards a place where they knew that many of their fellows resided. In 1971, there were 14,630 people from the Indian subcontinent and another 5,585 from the West Indies and Africa. By 1981, of 66,488 people in Southall, 25,690 were from the Commonwealth. In 1991, the overall population had fallen to 61,160, but the numbers of Indians and Pakistanis had risen to 35,214, and were mostly concentrated in the south and west of Southall, in Glebe, Northcote and Mount Pleasant wards.

Although Sikhs from the Punjab are the largest group in Southall, there were other groups of immigrants in this period. East African Asians from Kenya arrived after 1967 and Ugandan Asians, forced to leave in 1972, arrived in Southall. Many of these new arrivals were Gujarati Hindus, and of middle-class backgrounds. Somalis and Afghans arrived in Southall in the 1990s. By 1991, there were also 138 Chinese, 3,033 black Caribbeans and 987 black Africans living in Southall. To say that Southall has one

Worshippers at the Hindu Temple, Lady Margaret Road, 1978.

Asian community is a gross simplification; it has many, as well as people from other nations.

Southall was probably chosen as a destination for immigrants because it was an industrial borough, and was not far from other industrial boroughs. Later, the proximity of Heathrow Airport may have been an additional factor. Of course, when one community was established, it attracted others, perhaps because it reflected a home-from-home and perhaps because most of the first immigrants were men and their families joined them later. Although industrial work was not particularly pleasant, the wages offered were good and coming to Britain did present new arrivals with the prospect of a better life and an escape from hardships at home.

Few white people would let their property to outsiders; the 1950s and early 1960s were the times when signs saying 'No Irish, no blacks, no children' could legally be exhibited. It was rumoured in the early 1960s that the spate of Indians buying properties led to the devaluation of property, but a survey discovered that this was untrue and noted that of all immigrant groups, the Indians and Pakistanis preferred to buy if possible. Rather, prices rose, because the immigrants were in urgent need of accommodation. By 1989, 70% of Asians in Southall were owner-occupiers compared to other ethnic groups, where the proportion was about half of the total.

Arriving in a foreign country is never easy. Testimony from local immigrants bears this out. An educated Indian woman from Kenya said, 'In this country we started feeling inferior; this complex was created by the attitude of the white people towards us. For example, if we were not able to pronounce their names correctly they laughed and mocked us'. Another immigrant to Southall recollected 'They were not even liking us to be their neighbours. It was a clash of cultures.' And another, 'When I first came to this country I was shocked at the difference of the weather, grey buildings, grey sky and dull clothes'. It should be remembered that the culture shock went both ways. In 1951, only about half of Britain's population had ever met someone of a different colour, and, of course, the immigrants were (initially at least) as different to them as they were to the new arrivals.

In 1957, the tenth anniversary of the granting of independence to India was marked by about 500 Indians in Southall Park, and soon afterwards, the Indian Workers' Association was formed. This was in order to counter anti-immigration bodies, such as the Southall Residents' Association, and to protect their rights as workers (there were no local Indian councillors). The IWA became an important voice for the immigrants over the years. They recommended that its members vote Labour because of the latter's anti-EEC stance and working class nature.

The IWA were involved in many other campaigns, the best known of which was opposing the ban on the wearing of the turban while riding a motorcycle.

Indian involvement in mainstream local politics was limited until the mid-1960s. Although two IWA candidates did consider standing in the 1964 election, they did not do so because the Southall Residents' Association would have had two candidates stand to oppose them. The first Indian councillor to sit on Ealing Council was Mr S.S. Gill, a Southall resident, who was one of the three representatives of Northcote ward in the later 1960s, as a member of the Labour Party. Indeed, he was the only Indian to represent part of Southall on Ealing Council for almost ten years. By the 1990s, Southall's councillors were mostly Indian men, and members of the Labour Party. The first Asian from Southall to become the mayor of the London Borough of Ealing was Councillor Pathak in 1987.

Reactions by the indigenous population were not, initially at least, very favourable. Kirwan, writing in 1965, thought that, 'Relations between Europeans and Indians have not on the whole been very cordial'. This was not helped by the fact that there were few points of social contact between Indians and Britons – many of the former worked in factories outside Southall (where Asian and white men worked together, tensions were far less acute). It seems that many white people sold up and moved elsewhere, judging by the census statistics. It is often stated that Southall is truly multicultural, truly diverse, but arguably, places like Hanwell could be said to be more so, with a dominant white population (including Irish and European people), with a mix of other races. Racial violence has not occurred in Hanwell on anything like the scale which it did in Southall. Perhaps the two main issues which the indigenous population felt unhappy about were overcrowding and education. The Southall Residents' Association was formed as a pressure group to lobby the Labour council against further immigration.

Sir Edward Boyle, Minister for Education in 1963, met local residents and listened to their concerns, one of which being that the children of immigrants were attending the Featherstone Road schools, outnumbering white children. In order to prevent segregation (which Civil Rights groups in the USA were then campaigning against), a policy of bussing was introduced, in order to ensure that the children of different races mixed together. This sensible policy, which was supported by the IWA, came to an end in 1978.

Politicians often tried to ignore the problem. During the 1964 general election campaign, Labour canvassers downplayed the issue of immigration, which was the biggest single issue locally, and blamed the Conservative government for local woes. In fact, George Pargiter,

Southall's MP, though he spoke against the 1962 Immigration Act, believed that Southall could not asborb any more immigrants, favouring dispersal in order to aid social assimilation. He believed that the immigrants should conform to English fashions and practices. Both main parties however, sought to avoid 'the racial issues as such' and spoke against racial discrimination. The party which, somewhat naturally, did not, was the British National Party (BNP) who also contested the seat, and who accused the mainstream parties for being out of touch with the common man. The result of the 1964 election was close: Pargiter won with 48% per cent of the vote, but the Conservative Miss Maddin scored 42%, and, more worryingly, the BNP with 9%.

The number of the indigenous people living in Southall dropped dramatically. In 1961, they were 50,588 out of 52,983, in 1981, 37,987 out of 66,488 and in 1991, 18,221 out of 61,160. It would appear that the old white population was dying off or moving away from the district. New blood was not arriving, perhaps partly because of the closure of some of the large-scale factories in the 1960s and '70s, perhaps because of the increasing immigrant population there.

It is also important to survey the new communities which were making their homes in Southall. Although many of the Indians initially accepted employment in factories doing unskilled work, such as at Woolf's Rubber Factory, many were educated and later took professional jobs in a number of different fields, as was noted in the first Indian Who's Who, published in 1979. These included Mr K.S. Takhar, who owned four restaurants in 1989.

Just as in the later nineteenth and early twentieth centuries, new churches and chapels were built to accommodate the growing population of worshippers, the immigrants built places for their own worship. Many of Southall's new citizens were Punjabi Sikhs. At first they hired halls for their monthly meetings, but they acquired a temple in Southall Green in 1963, which was demolished four years later. A former dairy in Havelock Road was converted into a temple in 1967, which was able to house more people. In its turn, it was replaced in the 1990s by a new multimillion-pound Gurdwara, the Sri Guru Singh Sabha Gurdwara. Another Sikh temple, though rather smaller, was housed in a former Methodist chapel on Villiers Road in 1969. This was the Guru Granth Gurdwara. In 1972 a new temple, Ramgarhia Sabha, was built on Oswald Road.

Although Sikhism is now the principal religion in Southall, we should not forget Islam, Hinduism and Ravidass. There is one mosque (founded in 1975 on Townsend Road, moving to Montague Way in 1985), one Ravidass temple (founded in 1980 on the Western Road) and two Hindi temples. The Vishwa Hindu Kendra on Lady Margaret Road (founded in 1985) was allegedly the scene of a miracle in 1995 when a statue of

Ganesh, an elephant-headed god, drank milk. The scientific research into this phenomenon was inconclusive. It should also be added that some immigrants were Christian and worshipped at the established churches.

The inquiry on Incorporation of Southall in 1935 had stated that, 'this town has a worthy history, though I fear I can adduce no evidence of any... blood-lettings having taken place here.' Writing over sixty years later, the evidence is all too easy to find. Trouble between elements of different races spilled out into open violence on a number of occasions, none of which served to enhance Southall's renown.

Firstly, in 1958, there were a number of reports of hooligans attacking property and making threats. These included youths throwing bottles and stones through the windows of houses on Hammond Road, making abusive telephone calls, gathering in an armed crowd outside Woolf's Rubber Factory, and possibly setting fire to an Indian restaurant. Both the local police and neighbouring forces were on full alert. They acted to break up the crowd outside the rubber factory, where the latter dispersed. They also broke up a fight between white youths and Indians, arresting a number from both groups and fining some of them. The official Indian response was stated as being passive resistance.

There were also disturbances in the 1960s and '70s. This time, local responses were far from passive. Times had changed and a new generation of Indians had emerged, forming the radical Southall Youth Movement in 1976 (following the murder of Gurdip Singh Chaggar). Unemployment may have helped heighten tensions, too (there were 1,559 unemployed in Southall in 1979, and of these 964 were of ethnic origin), as well as the perceived hostility of the police (some spoke of a racist conspiracy). In

Police take cover, 1979.

Tariq Ali and Vishnu Sharma at an Anti-Front demonstration, 1979.

Police and demonstrators during the National Front rally in Southall, 1979.

1979, the National Front decided to ask that their right of free speech be upheld and that they be allowed to hold a meeting at Southall Town Hall. Unlike the case in 1938, with the BUF and the Park, the Ealing council allowed them to proceed. Such a provocative gesture by the NF did not go unheeded, and a counter-demonstration of local people and extreme left-wingers from elsewhere went ahead. The police, including the Special Forces Patrol Group, were out in force and, perhaps predictably, violence was the result. Mr Blair Peach, a socialist teacher from London's East End who was involved in the counter-demonstration, was killed, and some of his associates, without any real evidence, blamed the police for this. The inquest found that Mr Peach died through misadventure.

On 3 July 1981, a group of skinheads came to Southall, on the pretext of attending a disco at the Hambrough Tavern, but made it their business to insult the locals. This resulted in a running battle, ending with massive police intervention. Nearly 100 people were injured, the Tavern was burnt down, and local businesses and council property were damaged. There were many arrests, but, when the cases were held at Hendon Court, few convictions.

The last three paragraphs paint a bleak picture of race relations in Southall, and the incidents mentioned above certainly grabbed national and local headlines. Yet they only represent a small part of the story. It should be noted that the troublemakers, whether gangs of hooligans in the late 1950s or skinheads and the National Front in later years, were outsiders, not locals. However, apart from these major incidents, there were many others, though on a lesser scale. Tensions lessened over the years, and in the summer of 2001 when there were race riots in some northern cities, there were none in Southall.

*Some Asian shops on
The Green, Southall,
1960s.*

Southall's shops were never particularly noteworthy, as has been mentioned in chapter six. In this period they were transformed and offered shoppers an experience that they could not really find elsewhere in London. Although most of Southall's shops were owned by the indigenous population in the 1960s, as the shopkeepers either died or left the district, the premises were taken over by the rising numbers of Asians. While there were only four Asian-owned food shops in Southall in 1964, the situation quickly changed. In 1971, according to one writer discussing Southall, the area has been 'given new life by immigrants who have actually made the place somewhere at least to shop'.

In the 1970s, Southall had its own Asian cinemas, travel agents, marriage bureaux, banks and insurance agents as well as shops. Bombay Halwa Ltd, makers of Royal sweets, began in business in 1899 in India and they set up shop in Southall in 1974. By the 1980s they were possibly the largest manufacturer of Asian sweets in the UK. In the 1980s other Indian businessmen moved into what were for them, new fields. One such was Mr J. Singh, director of Audio Link Services, repairing electronic goods.

Apart from the shops, there are also Indian restaurants and an Indian pub. In 1999, there were thirty-five restaurants, many of which were on the Broadway or South Road. The latter, The Glassy Junction, is run by Punjabis and has a strong Indian atmosphere, with Asian music and dance sessions. The interior décor includes paintings of Indian dancers. Indian currency is accepted as payment for drinks in this establishment.

Hanwell's shops had always been sufficient for basic needs. In the 1970s there were many small shops of all varieties; small supermarkets, several butchers and grocers, shops selling electrical goods and shoe repairers, for example. Many were situated in the Broadway and on Boston Road. One

Gem Cinema, Southall Green, c.1950.

Hanwell Carnival, 1969.

resident remarked, 'You could buy anything'. However, in the 1980s, three changes occurred which spelt the closing of some of these shops and general decline. Firstly, the opening of the supermarkets Sainsbury's and Waitrose in West Ealing in the 1980s drew business away from the smaller shops in Hanwell. Secondly, the closing of the sub-post office in the Boston Road resulted in people who drew benefits from there having to go (and shop) elsewhere. Finally, the bus depot closed in 1990, which helped to reduce custom for these shops still further. Furthermore, by the 1990s, there were no branches of any banks in Hanwell. The result was that many of the shops closed, reducing Hanwell's appeal as a place for local people to shop.

In the 1970s, comments about Hanwell and Southall were generally unfavourable, the idea being that both districts were rather run-down. A guide aimed at potential home owners and tenants in London, published in 1971, dismissed the two districts thus: 'No special attraction' and 'The seamy side of old Middlesex', giving each a very poor summing-up. However, many of the problems were symptomatic of a wider malaise. These problems included overcrowding, poor housing, industrial decline, the closing down of familiar landmarks and, perhaps most visibly, litter on the streets.

Southall, once known as an industrial centre, suffered from closures in the late 1960s and '70s as national recessions bit. Firms which closed included the Woolf factory in 1967, Arrow Switches in 1968, the Gasworks in 1973, Cramic Engineering in 1978 and AEC in 1979. The result was that Southall's unemployment was disproportionately higher than elsewhere. In 1976, when the unemployment rate in Greater London was 3.7%, in the Northcote ward in Southall it was 6.7%. In 1980, when unemployment in outer London was 3.86%, it was 10% in Southall. One study in 1981 concluded that, 'Southall is a town in decline'. In 1991, 15% of the working population lacked jobs.

There has been some economic and commercial revival in Southall. It is arguable that, to an extent, Southall has become a centre of large-scale capitalist enterprise once more. In *Asian Enterprise and the Regeneration of Britain*, written in 1989, it was stated, 'Southall is really the repository of big Asian business.' This is an ambitious statement, but the facts seem to bear it out. In 1980 the Southbridge Trading Estate opened, and one of the success stories was that of the four Sutterwalla Brothers. Beginning with a small wholesale grocery outlet, two years later they employed 125 people and had an annual turnover that year of £12 million. Another big business

Brentside Middle School, Kennedy Road, 1976.

was founded in 1987 by the four Rudki brothers. This was C&L (London Ltd), a textile company, which was an offshoot of their father's company. The two companies have an annual turnover of £9 million (1989). Mr Biji, a Kenyan businessman who arrived in Southall in 1985, and bought premises at the Barrat Industrial Park. He imports food from Uganda, Kenya and India, then supplies it to grocers all over the UK. Another successful Southall entrepreneur is Atvar Lit, chief executive of Sunrise radio station (founded 1989). Finally, there is Noon Products, which prepares frozen Indian food for many major supermarkets in the UK and for British Airways.

In Hanwell, community spirit was manifested in the formation of the Hanwell Preservation Society, a group of middle-class activists, concerned about the quality of life in Hanwell that was perceived to be under threat. The group was formed in 1971 and over the next two decades campaigned on a number of local issues. These included; pollution in the River Brent and the preservation of the Victorian railway station. They collaborated with the council over the formation of the Hanwell Village Conservation Area. The Group was dissolved in 1990, but were replaced by the Hanwell Steering Group in that year. In 2000 the Hanwell History Society was established.

Hanwell Carnival, held each summer in Elthorne Park, beginning in 1960, became a focus for local loyalties. In 1976, its president, Mr G.S.C. Durtnal wrote that it was, 'The most important date in our local Community's Calendar'. John Price, a Texan vicar who spent several months in Hanwell in this year wrote glowingly of the district. He wrote, 'Hanwell retains its identity despite the faceless imposed reboundary-ing, Hanwellians have a spirit about them which is noticeable to the outsider.'

There were moves to create conservation areas within the Borough of Ealing in 1969 where planning controls were to be tighter than elsewhere in the borough. For the purposes of this book, the relevant ones are Norwood Green and Churchfields, Hanwell. Hanwell Village Green Conservation Area was later added to the list. The council aims to counter the threats to these areas by alleviating problems caused by traffic and inappropriate street furniture, for example, which would otherwise erode their character.

Many of the houses in south Hanwell in the 1960s and '70s were rented properties, and some had not been well cared for either by landlords or tenants. Although they could have been pleasant dwellings with gardens, many looked run-down. A housing survey taken in 1968-1969 of nearly a thousand properties in Hanwell to the south of the Uxbridge Road, revealed that nearly half lacked one to five basic household amenities. Street parking, by residents and by commercial vehicles, resulted in heavy congestion. Conditions were especially bad around the southern part of the area, next to an industrial estate. Fumes, heavy traffic, vibrations, noise and smell all contributed to make the area unpleasant. Domestic garages, tree planting and open play areas were too few in number. Some poorer residents resisted plans for change because it would mean that their landlords could increase their rents.

Southall and Hanwell have changed a great deal in the fifty years since the end of the Second World War. Change is inevitable, and that in Southall was far more dramatic than that in Hanwell. Hanwell has seen some decline especially as regards its shops, but has also preserved its essential environment – as one long-standing resident remarked, he would never think of leaving and mentioned the open spaces as a major factor in this decision. Southall has become home to the largest Indian population in London, with its temples and mosques co-existing with the existing churches and chapels. Asian entrepreneurial ability has certainly helped rejuvenate Southall, though unemployment in 2001 was at a higher level than the borough average and illegal drug-taking was a concern.

It is usual for a local historian to end on a suitable valedictory note. Since predictions of future joy or misery are only given to astrologers, I shall not attempt to emulate them, but will only offer a very short summary of the book.

Over the centuries, Hanwell and Southall have grown from being two small Saxon settlements in Middlesex to becoming part of the large suburban sprawl of western London. However, for much of their history, until the nineteenth century, they were rural and agricultural. Industrial and suburban growth occurred slowly, as transport improved and because space was available for expansion. Both are part of a larger borough and will undoubtedly be so for the foreseeable future. Whether this is a mixed blessing remains to be seen.

Walking Tour

This is a circular route which can be walked as a whole, or can be broken up into two halves, depending on the time available and on the walkers' level of fitness and enthusiasm. There are two suggestions made in the text to shorten the distance. The complete walk takes around five hours, plus time for breaks. Please note that this walking tour does not incorporate all the historic sights in Southall and Hanwell. It very much focuses on the central parts of these two districts, for the simple reason that this is where most of the older and interesting buildings are – in the opinion of this author – to be found. Listed buildings are noted by the number in brackets. Locally listed buildings are marked thus (*).

> **The walk begins outside the Kensington Cemetery on the Uxbridge Road, Hanwell.**

This cemetery was opened in 1855, having been built by Thomas Allom, and is open most days. It was built because of the overcrowding in churchyards in central London, and in particular, the churchyard of St Mary's, Kensington. Mid-nineteenth century legislation decreed that central London churchyards should be closed because of the danger to public health and that the dead be buried outside the metropolis.

> **Continue westwards.**

Soon you will see the Westminster Cemetery, opened in 1854, on the left-hand side of the road. This cemetery was opened in 1854 and was initially used to bury the dead of St George's, Hanover Square. The architect was Robert Jerrard.

> **Continue walking westwards until you reach St Joseph's Catholic church on the left.**

There has been a Catholic church on this site since 1865. The present building, Our Lady and St Joseph, was built in 1964-1967; the architects were Reynolds and Scott. Pevsener refers to its roof as being, 'a horrible jagged outline of concrete dormers'.

Walking Tour

> *Cross the Uxbridge Road carefully, using the traffic lights. Walk northwards up Church Road. On your immediate left is St Mellitus' church.*

St Mellitus' church was built in 1909-1910, and was the first Anglican church in Hanwell to be assigned a parish out of the ancient parish of St Mary's. The new parish was formed out of the area between the railway line and Elthorne Park. It is named after St Mellitus, the Saxon bishop, who, according to Sharpe, converted the Saxons of Hanwell to Christianity. It was designed by Sir Arthur Blomfield and Sons in the Gothic style.

> *Walking up Church Road, the Methodist church is on your right.*

The Methodist church, on Church Road, was built in 1904, the architects being Gordon and Gunton. Previous Methodist churches in Hanwell had been located in the Lower Boston Road, on the corner with St Dunstan's Road.

> *Continue walking up Church Road, which bends to the left. Just after walking under the railway bridge, turn left into Campbell Road. At the end of the road is the railway station.*

Hanwell railway station (2) was once known as Hanwell and Elthorne station. There has been a railway station here since 1838. It was rebuilt in 1875-1877 and, unlike many others, has retained its essentially mid-Victorian appearance. Even for those who are not transport enthusiasts, there is much here to enjoy.

> *Once you have seen all that you want to, return to Campbell Road and retrace your steps to Church Road. Keep following this road, which winds to the left. The Recreation Ground is on the left, and on the right is The Hermitage.*

The Hermitage (2) is a delightful early nineteenth-century thatched cottage, built on the site of an earlier building, Elm Haw, shortly after 1809. It is

Walking Tour

probable that Revd George Glasse had the new property built. In 1861 it was the home of Edmund Spearman, a civil servant, his wife, child and five servants.

> *Eventually you will reach the end of the road and the Parish church is on the right.*

St Mary's Parish church (2). Although there may have been a church on this site in Saxon times, the first recorded church dates from the twelfth century. The present building is the third church, built in 1841 and consecrated the following year. It was one of the first churches designed by George Gilbert Scott. Scott was one of the leading architects of the Victorian era; another local church which he designed is Christ the Saviour, on Ealing Broadway.

> *To the left of the church is Churchfields Recreation Ground. Enter it and walk down the main avenue.*

Churchfield Recreation Ground was the first of Hanwell's parks, opened in 1898. To the right of the main walkway through the park is a small memorial to the former Boy Scouts who fell during the First World War, and nearby, is an even smaller marker to the Revd George Glasse. You will also see from here the north side of the Wharncliffe Viaduct, and of that, more anon.

> *On leaving the Park, proceed to the left and then turn right along Campbell Road.*

On the wall of No. 8 is a blue plaque to W.F. Yeames, the artist mentioned in chapter five, who lived here from 1894-1912.

> *Continue along Campbell Road. The railway station will be seen on the right. At this point, some may prefer to take the train one stop westwards to Southall station. This will cut at least an hour from the walk and miss out the most tedious part, but it will also mean missing out some of the landmarks as described below (though Hanwell Bridge and the old gates of the County asylum will be fleetingly glimpsed from the train). If this is the preferred option, go to page 124.*

Walking Tour

Assuming one wishes to proceed, at the end of Campbell Road, turn right back into Church Road. After passing under the railway bridge, take the second right, Cherington Road.

There are two places on this road, both on the right-hand side which are of interest. The first is the Hanwell Carnegie Library, which was opened in 1905 and is still in use as a library. Its first librarian was Frank Pocock, who was killed on the Western Front in 1918.

The second is Cherington House (*). It is unclear exactly how old this building is. Certainly it would seem to date from the early nineteenth century, but is first definitely recorded in 1861. It takes its name from the place of birth of its owner of that year. Hanwell Local Board, founded in 1886, met in hired rooms until the winter of 1891-1892, when this building was purchased for use as council offices. It is now used as a health centre.

Walk down Cherington Road and you will enter Hanwell Broadway.

On your left is a striking Art Deco feature. This is the Coronation Clock Tower, which was built to celebrate the coronation of George VI in May 1937. It was built by Ealing Council, though it was a Hanwell councillor who pushed to have it built in the first place. It was restored to mark the Golden Jubilee of the King's daughter, Elizabeth II, in 2002.

Walk westwards and there are two of Hanwell's oldest pubs on your right. If you are thirsty, they are worth stopping at.

The first is The Duke of York, dating back to at least 1826. It was probably named after George III's second son who is famous as the Grand Old Duke of York in the nursery rhyme, though he was a competent military administrator as Commander in Chief of the British Army during the Napoleonic Wars. Stagecoaches collected passengers from here in the 1830s.

A little further down the road, as it begins to slope downwards towards the river, is the next pub.

Walking Tour

The Viaduct pub (*) was known as The Coach and Horses until about 1838. It takes its current name from the Wharncliffe Viaduct, of course. There has been a bridge (2) at this point for centuries – at least since the Middle Ages. Readers of this book will be aware that it has had to be repaired or rebuilt many times throughout the ages. The present structure possesses a nineteenth-century stone balustrade and there are eighteenth-century brick arches on its west side.

> *Cross the bridge and continue up the slight incline. To the left is the southern aspect of the Viaduct.*

The Wharncliffe Viaduct (1) was built in 1836-1838 from a design by Isambard Kingdom Brunel – his first major building project. It takes its name from the chairman of the Parliamentary committee which steered the GWR Bill through Parliament. His coat of arms can be seen in outline on the side of the viaduct. The viaduct was doubled in width in 1877. According to Pevsener, 'Few viaducts have such architectural panache'.

> *On the left is what is now Ealing Hospital.*

The large glass modern structure was built between the late 1960s and the '80s. The former County asylum (2) was constructed between 1829 and 1831, though there were many extensions through the nineteenth century. It became later known as St Bernard's Hospital and is now Ealing Hospital. This hospital also replaces the general King Edward Memorial Hospital, which was situated on Mattock Lane, Ealing. Much of the original structure is gone, though the imposing gateway remains, as does part of the blocks.

> *Carry on westwards. You will now be approaching an iron bridge which crosses the main road.*

This is the Iron Bridge. The original was built in about 1838, but burned down in 1847. The present structure is built of wrought iron. It carries the main line from London to Bristol.

> *Carry on westwards. The walk here is quite long. On the right is Dormers Wells Lane, which is the site of the Tudor manor house, of which there is now no visible trace. Eventually you will see Holy Trinity church on the right.*

The church was built here in 1890 by John Lee and was opened in the following year. From 1869-1889, an iron building had been used as the place of worship; its location was on the site of the town hall. William Welch Deloitte, founder of the great accountancy firm which still bears his name, was Churchwarden here from 1869-1889.

> **On the left is Southall Park.**

Southall Park was once part of an estate surrounding a large house of the same name. It was used as a private lunatic asylum from 1839-1883, first by Sir William Ellis, then by Lady Ellis, and last of all by Robert Boyd. The asylum burnt to the ground in 1883, killing the owner and five others. The site was bought by the council in 1909, a lake being constructed there in 1923. It has been the setting for coronation and jubilee celebrations and other national rejoicing, and for carnivals and festivals.

> **Continue to walk westwards. On the left is the Red Lion public house.**

There has been a Red Lion (2) pub in Southall since the seventeenth century. Parts of the present structure date from the eighteenth century.

> **Carry on walking ahead. Eventually, a crossroads will be reached. Just before the crossroads, on the right, stands Southall Town Hall.**

Southall Town Hall (*) was built in 1897 at a cost of £9,000, to house the offices of Southall-Norwood Urban District Council, and was also the headquarters of Southall Borough until its abolition in 1965. Latterly it has been used by the council as a careers and advice centre.

> **At the crossroads turn left into South Road, one of Southall's busiest thoroughfares. Along this road are many shops whose wares are on stalls in the street. After you have passed St Joseph's Drive on the right, you will see the King's Hall.**

Walking Tour

King's Hall, Methodist chapel (*) was built in 1916. The architect was Sir Michael Gelder of Hull. In 1952, Elizabeth Schwarzkopf and Kathleen Ferrier sang here as part of the council's celebrity concerts.

> *Continue southwards. On the left is the Asian pub, the Glassy Junction. Then we reach the railway bridge. On crossing the railway, there are several sites worth noting, and this is a good place from which to view them.*

Firstly, there is the railway station on the left. Although a stop was established here in 1839, a station was not built for another twenty years. It was once an important point for the movement of industrial goods from Brentford Docks and elsewhere. It's name has been printed in two languages since 1998. Secondly, there is the Water Tower (2), Southall's 'Castle', which from 1895-1968 supplied water for the trains using the station. It has since been converted for use as flats. Thirdly, from this vantage point there is the Gasworks, built in around 1865. The gasometer has the initials 'LH' on its side, an indicator for aircraft as they fly towards Heathrow. Finally, looking to the left can be seen the building which was built as the Maypole Institute (see chapter six).

> *At the roundabout, carry on following the main road, which becomes The Green, veering ever so slightly to the south west. After a couple of minutes, on your left is Osterley Park Road. If you walk down this road you will see the town's library.*

Southall Library is another Carnegie library. It was opened in 1905 by the wife of James Bigwood, the local MP. The Art Nouveau lettering above the door and the triple arch entrance are most attractive.

> *Shortly after this minor diversion, return to The Green. Continue walking southwards and on your left you will see what many think to be the most important building in Southall. This is the Manor House.*

Southall Manor House (2) is now dwarfed by the surrounding buildings, but it is still impressive. It must have been even moreso in the sixteenth century. Although there was an earlier building on the site, Richard

Awsiter, lord of the manor, decided to have it rebuilt in about 1587. Over the centuries, it has seen many alterations and much rebuilding, yet much of the original half-timbered Elizabethan structure remains. It has had many owners over the years. In 1913 it fell into the council's hands and was used as a health centre. By 1970 there was a danger that the building might be demolished, but it was saved by the local chamber of commerce who used it as their headquarters. It is hoped that its future safety is now assured. Few manor houses of this date survive so close to London.

> *Apart from looking at the Manor House and its grounds, notice the War memorial.*

The war memorial was unveiled on 8 April 1922 by the local MP, Colonel Sidney Peel. A new set of dates was added after 1945 to commemorate the Second World War.

> *Carry on walking down the main road as it turns into King Street. On the right-hand side of the road are the Hindu temple and St John's church. A little further on , on the left of the road, along Havelock Road is a new and huge Sikh temple, Gurdwara Sri Guru Singh Sabha. On reaching Norwood Road, turn left and walk down the road, crossing Wolf Bridge, continuing on that road until reaching Norwood Road.*

The contrast between the Indian shops and temples of South Road and King Street and the rather leafy Norwood is remarkable; nineteenth-century writers commented on the tedious streets of Southall with the country mansions of Norwood.

> *Walk along this new road and then turn left into Tentelow Lane. On the left are a number of interesting buildings. To take them in order:*

Norwood Hall, (*) once Norwood Lodge, was built in 1801-1803 by John Soane for his friend and business associate, John Robbins, estate agent and auctioneer. It has later been used as a horticultural college.

St Mary's church (2) has stood on this site since the twelfth century and there may have been an earlier Saxon church. Parts of the church are Norman, but there has been, as with all old buildings, much rebuilding over the centuries. There were some changes in the early fifteenth century due to Archbishop Chicele's intervention, and there was also major work in the 1860s, including replacing the old spire with a tower. Inside the church there are numerous monuments to former parishioners. These include: Edward Cheseman (died 1509), John Merrick,(died 1749) and Francis Awsiter (died 1624).

The Biscoe School was founded in 1767 and is described in chapter two. There is a faded white plaque on this building.

> *After leaving these buildings, walk up Tentelow Lane. This is qute a lengthy road of suburban dwellings. Carry on walking up Tenlelow Lane, until you reach the junction. Windmill Bridge is on the left. Cross the bridge, while looking at the views.*

The Three Bridges (2) was designed by Brunel in order that the railway branch line from Southall to Brentford could pass beneath both the existing canal and Windmill Lane. It was one of his last pieces of work, being accomplished in 1859, the year of his death. This canal was called the Grand Junction Canal from 1794 until 1928, when it and all the other canals around London were called the Grand Union Canal. This part of the canal eventually leads to the Thames.

> *There are two choices as to how to end the walk. One is to walk up Windmill Lane and then, on returning to the Uxbridge Road, to walk eastwards back towards Hanwell. The other, and preferred route, is to walk by the canal, via the opening to the right of the bridge.*

This is a short walk, in which the oft-painted Hanwell Top Locks is seen on the right. On the left is the hospital, surrounded by a high wall. There is a bricked-up arched section; this was formerly part of the docks where barges brought supplies to the asylum and left with finished goods made by the inmates.

> *After passing Hanwell Lock 96, turn left. On the right is the River Brent (which joins the canal), to the left is the hospital. From there, walk up the pathway to Hanwell Bridge, near to where this walk began. You are near to the Viaduct pub and have earned a pint. Cheers!*

Bibliography

N.B. All sources are located at Ealing Local History Centre unless otherwise stated.

Primary Sources

S. McAlpine, ed., *Voices of Ealing and Hounslow* (2000)

Transcripts of St Mary's Norwood Parish Registers

Diary of John Hull Grundy (1920s)

Diary of Henry St John (1940s)

Diary of Charles Burton (1833-1834)

Middlesex maps (sixteenth and seventeenth century)

Rocque Map (1741-5)

Ordnance Survey Maps (1865-1935)

Census digests, 1921-1991

Census Returns, 1841-1891

Calendars of State Papers Domestic (sixteenth and seventeenth centuries) [Public Record Office]

The 68th report of the visiting justices to the County Lunatic Asylum at Hanwell, (1843)

Middlesex and Brentford Petty Sessions Calendars (sixteenth to eighteenth centuries) [London Metropolitan Archives]

Hanwell Gazette, 1894-1923

Middlesex County Times

Southall News, 1885-1888

Southall Gazette

West Middlesex Gazette

Southall-Norwood Gazette

School logbooks for St Ann's, Hanwell, Oaklands Road Infants, Hanwell, Clifton Road, Southall.

Southall Borough Guides, 1926-1965

Ealing Borough Guides, 1965-1990

Middlesex Poll Books (eighteenth century)

Hanwell Inventories (seventeenth century) [London Metropolitan Archives]

Surprise Yourself in Southall (1999)

Norwood Valuations, 1821, 1863.

Norwood Overseers and Churchwardens' Accounts (seventeenth and eighteenth centuries)

Hanwell Vestry Minutes (eighteenth century)

Kelly's directories, 1887-1940

Middlesex directories, 1826-1937

The Gentleman's Magazine (eighteenth century)

Secondary Sources

M. Briggs, *Middlesex Old and New*, (1934)

J. Cameron, *Unemployment in Southall*, (1981)

N. Deakin, *Colour and the General Election of 1964*, (1965)

A. Faulkner, *The Grand Junction Canal*, (1972)

P. Hounsell, *Ealing and Hanwell Past*, (1991)

P. Hounsell, *The brick-making industry in West Middlesex*, PhD thesis, 2000

P. Kirwan, *Southall: A Brief History*, (1965)

D. Lysons, *Middlesex, Vols. II and III*, (1795)

K. McEwan, *Ealing Walkabout*, (1984)

R.J. Meads, *Southall, 830-1982*, (1983)

R.J. Meads, *Growing up in Southall from 1904*, (1979)

R.J. Meads, *The Maypole and the Green*, (1980)

G. Meason, *The Illustrated Guide to the Great Western Railway, 1852*, (1985)

C. Neaves, *Greater Ealing*, (1931)

H.A. Norris, *The Hanwell Asylum, St Bernard's Hospital*, (1983)

J. Oates, *Southall: The Archive Photographs*, (2001)

N. Pevenser, *The Buildings of England, London North West*, (1991)

M. Sharpe, *Middlesex in British, Roman and Saxon Times*, (1919)

M. Sharpe, *Bygone Hanwell and the chapelry of old Brentford*, (1924)

J. Simmons, ed., *The Birth of the Great Western Railway*, (1971)

J. Thorne, *Environs of London*, (1876)

G. Twyman, *The Martin Brothers*, (1995)

D. Upton, *The dangerous years*, (1993)

C.E. Vulliamy, *The County Archaeologies: Middlesex and London*, (1930)

E. Walford, *Greater London*, (1882)

P. Whitehouse and D. St John Thomas, *The Great Western Railway*, (1984)

Asian Enterprise and the regeneration of Britain, (1989)

Victoria County History for Middlesex, Vols III and IV.

Southall Local History Society Transactions, 1959-1965

London and Middlesex Archaeological Transactions

Index